Scandinavian Cooking

Recipes from Sweden, Norway, Denmark and Finland,
selected and tested by the Wezäta test kitchen
Crown Publishers, Inc., New York

ISBN 0-517-526190
First published in the U.S.A. 1976
by Crown Publishers, Inc.
One Park Avenue
New York, New York 10016.

Library of Congress Catalog
Card Number: 76-2215

Design: Curt Svenson

Printed in Sweden by Wezäta, Gothenburg, 1977

Open-faced sandwiches

Smörgåsbord

4

Sandwiches

As you can see from the picture open-faced sandwiches can be decorated in many different ways. These are only a few examples of how you can get open-faced sandwiches in Scandinavia. The ingredients on these sandwiches are from left:

Cod roe cakes coated with bread crumbs and fried, topped with curried mayonnaise and garnished with slices of lemon and fresh dill.

Slices of bacon, topped with celery salad.

Mixed chicken salad, topped with garden cress, pieces of chicken and red pepper.

Slices of lunch meat, topped with vegetable mayonnaise and garnished with a slice of egg and parsley.

Generously cut slices of Scandinavian cheese.

Roast beef slices, topped with rémoulade sauce and garnished with fried onion and cucumbers.

Jansson's temptation
4 servings

This is one of the simplest and very best of the traditional smörgåsbord dishes. All it requires is Scandinavian anchovies—and they may be hard to find. But if you have a source for them you can stock up on them; anchovies improve with age and can be kept for a year in the refrigerator. Jansson's temptation is an excellent party dish and a very good appetizer by itself. It has a mild, slightly salty taste—and it's not a bit fishy, unlike most of the other herring or smelt dishes.

5 medium-sized raw potatoes
2 onions
1 small can (3 oz) of Scandinavian anchovies
a mixture of table cream and juice from the anchovies to make ⅔—1 cup (2 dl) of liquid
2 tbsp butter

Preheat oven to 400—450°. Peel potatoes and cut into narrow strips, like French fries. Peel and chop onions. Chop anchovies. Butter a low ovenware dish and layer potatoes, onions and anchovies, with a layer of potatoes on top. Pour half the liquid on top. Bake for about 20 minutes. Pour in remaining liquid and bake till potatoes are tender (another 30 minutes). Serve hot or lukewarm.

The open-faced sandwich is a Scandinavian specialty. In its simplest form it is served every day in almost every home, for breakfast, for lunch, as an after-school snack, and for supper. More elaborate

Meatballs
4 servings

*Meatballs used to be made of a mixture
of ground beef and ground lean pork, sometimes with the addition of ground veal.
If you want to make classic meatballs, you
may have to grind your own pork. But
ground lean beef by itself will do very
nicely too.*

*Meatballs are a simple dish. There are no
herbs, no fancy sauces, no sour cream, no
tomatoes. If they are served on a smörgåsbord
or as an appetizer they can be either cold
or hot. As a main dish they can be served
with gravy made from the drippings in
the pan with an addition of stock, bouillon
cubes or soy sauce. The smaller the meatballs,
the finer they are. For a smörgåsbord they're
usually the size of a quarter, or smaller.*

*Cook small meatballs about 5 minutes,
larger ones about 8 minutes. Roll meatballs
with your hands. If you keep your hands
wet and put the finished meatballs on
a moistened cutting board, they're easy to
handle. There is a trick to frying them and
keeping them round. The butter should be
hot. Don't fill the skillet more than two-
thirds full. Shake frequently so that the
meatballs roll around in the hot butter and
are browned on all sides.*

*Turn heat down and let them cook through.
If you fry a lot of meatballs, the skillet may
have to be washed (and thoroughly dried)
between every two or three batches. Meatballs freeze very well. If you make gravy,
the gravy should be frozen separately.*

1 lb (450 g) ground meat (beef and pork
    mixed or beef only)
1 egg
1½ tsp salt
dash of pepper
(dash of allspice)
⅓ — ½ cup (1 dl) unseasoned bread crumbs
¾ cup (2 dl) table cream or milk
1 medium-sized onion
butter

Peel and grate onion. The grated onion can
be fried or used raw, as you prefer. Raw
onion gives a somewhat stronger taste. Soak
bread crumbs in cream. Mix meat, egg,
spices and grated onion. Add bread crumbs
to meat mixture, and stir well. Roll meatballs and fry in a generous amount of hot
butter.

varieties are served as hors d'oeuvre or party
dishes. The Danes are the sandwich experts. They
turn sandwiches into gourmet treats, masterpieces
of taste and looks. Many small Danish restaurants

Bird's nest

1 raw egg yolk
2 tbsp capers
3 tbsp chopped onion
1 small can (3 oz) Scandinavian anchovy
   fillets, finely chopped
3 tbsp pickled beets, finely chopped
3 tbsp parsley, finely chopped

Place a small glass upside down on a plate.
Arrange capers in a ring around the glass,
then add rings of chopped onions, anchovies,
beets and parsley. Remove glass and slide
the raw egg yolk into the middle. Serve
immediately — the egg yolk dries if it's
left standing. To eat, mix the ingredients on
the plate and spread on a piece of bread.

Old man's delight
4 servings

*An odd name and a strange concoction
which is part of every true smörgåsbord.
Maybe its consistency, like soft mush, was
particularly suited for old people; maybe
they liked its strong salty flavor which goes
so well with a glass of aquavit.*

5 fillets of Scandinavian anchovies
2 hard-boiled eggs
1 large onion
2—3 tbsp butter

Chop anchovies and hard-boiled eggs. Grate
or chop onion finely. Mix ingredients and fry
them in butter. Serve hot, topped with finely
chopped parsley.

serve only sandwiches for luncheon. Scandinavian
sandwiches are always tasteful and appetizing. They
are not hard to make. Once you get the knack of it
you will find many ways to improve and vary them.

Mushroom-filled tomatoes

Stuffed eggs

8 medium-sized tomatoes
salt
pepper

Stuffing:
2 tbsp butter
½ lb (250 g) chopped mushrooms,
fresh or canned
1 cup (2 dl) liquid, table cream and stock
(if canned mushrooms are used)
salt
pepper
1 tbsp dry sherry
2 tbsp grated cheese

Preheat oven to 375°. Wash tomatoes and cut off the top. Scoop out the center and sprinkle the inside with salt and pepper. Melt butter and sauté mushrooms over low heat. Season. Stir in flour and add liquid gradually. Simmer 5 minutes, stirring. Season and add wine. Place tomatoes in buttered baking dish and fill with creamed mushrooms. Sprinkle top with cheese. Bake for about 15 minutes or until golden brown.

Cod roe spread is only available in Scandinavian grocery stores.

4 hard-boiled eggs
1 tbsp butter
3 tbsp Scandinavian caviar
(cod roe spread)
salt
pepper

Garnish:
parsley
tomatoes
lettuce

Cut eggs into halves crosswise or lengthwise. Remove yolks carefully and put whites aside. Mix egg yolks, butter and caviar and stir until smooth. Season to taste. Force through pastry bag into whites. Decorate each egg with a sprig of parsley. Arrange on platter on lettuce leaves and garnish with sliced tomatoes.

Admittedly, they are harder to eat than the average American sandwich. You can't eat a mound of shrimps topped with mayonnaise and dill on a wafer-thin slice of bread with your fingers. The more elabo-

Mustard marinated smelt
4 servings

This is an intriguing, spicy and quite eco-nomical dish. Often, as in this dish, the smelt is eaten raw (so is matjes herring or any other pickled herring). Don't let that deter you. Marinated smelt is well worth the effort and a very good appetizer. Served with hot boiled potatoes it becomes a small entrée.

1 lb (500 g) fillets of smelt

Marinade:
1¾ cup (4 dl) water
⅔ cup (1½ dl) pickling vinegar
1 tbsp salt

Dressing:
½ cup (1 dl) mustard
4 tbsp vinegar
½ cup (1 dl) oil
2 tbsp sugar
½ tsp coarsely ground pepper
½ cup (1 dl) chopped fresh dill

The smelt will probably be frozen. Let it thaw and skin it; peel off a little piece of the skin with a sharp knife, grasp it with a piece of paper towel and pull; it should come off easily. Cut fillets in halves. Mix marinade and pour over fish in a large bowl. Marinate in refrigerator over night. Mix ingredients for dressing. Drain fillets and layer them with dressing in a wide-mouthed jar or crock. Chill for at least 24 hours before serving.

Smelt in tomato marinade
4 servings

1 lb (500 g) fillets of smelt
2 tsp salt
½ cup (1 dl) fresh chopped dill
2 tsp dill seeds
½ cup (1 dl) tomato purée, thinned with
¼ cup (½ dl) water

Thaw fillets. Season with salt and dill seeds and roll them with the meaty side out, or skin side out as in Finland. Pack the rolled fish tightly into a low wide pan. The rolls should support each other and keep their shape. Fasten with toothpicks if they don't hold together. Sprinkle remaining dill seeds and fresh dill over them and pour in tomato purée thinned with water. Cover and simmer over low heat for 10 minutes or until fish is done. Serve cold as an appetizer or hot as a main dish together with boiled potatoes and a salad.

rate Scandinavian sandwich, except for tiny bit-sized cocktail sandwiches, is always served with a knife and fork. Beer, wine, coffee, tea, milk, or any other drink can be served with the sandwiches.

Pickled smelt

1 lb (500 g) smelt
butter
5 tbsp tomato purée
¾ cup (2 dl) oil
⅓ cup (1 dl) pickling vinegar
3 tsp salt
½ tsp pepper

Preheat oven to 425°. Clean and rinse the
smelt but leave the backbone. Butter an
ovenware dish and put the smelt in it. Mix
the other ingredients and pour them over
the smelt. Cover with foil and cook for
about 20 minutes. Serve cool.

Danish herring salad
6—8 servings

*Put fillets in cold water over night,
rinse and dry before using.*

4—6 fillets of salt herring
2 medium-sized potatoes, boiled and cold
2 pickled beets
1 sour pickle
2 medium-sized tart apples
1 small red onion

Dressing:
2 tbsp butter
2 tbsp flour
1⅓ cup (3 dl) table cream
2 tbsp juice of pickled beets
1 tsp mustard
½ tsp pepper
(sugar)

Garnish:
2 hard-boiled eggs
parsley

Start by making the dressing. Melt butter and
blend in flour over low heat. Slowly stir in
table cream. Keep stirring till sauce has
thickened, then simmer for 3—4 minutes.
Remove from heat and add vinegar, mustard
and salt (plus a little bit of sugar if you like).
Cool. Now peel apples and potatoes. Chop all
the ingredients and mix into cold dressing.
Serve in a bowl, garnished with sliced hard-
boiled eggs and sprigs of parsley.

Smörgåsbord means literally "a table of sandwiches".
At first the smörgåsbord consisted only of a few
snacks which were served as an appetizer together
with a glass of aquavit, a strong Scandinavian liquor.

Grandmother's herring
6—8 servings

4—6 fillets of salt herring
1 cup (2½ dl) chopped leek or spring onions
3—4 tbsp chopped cocktail onions

Dressing:
⅔ cup (1½ dl) mayonnaise
⅓ cup (1 dl) sour cream
1 tsp curry
1 tsp paprika

Soak salt herring over night. Drain and cut into small pieces. Layer the herring with chopped leek and onions in a bowl or any other suitable dish — in Scandinavian countries a wide-mouthed jar is often used. Pour dressing over it. Marinate 24 hours in refrigerator before serving.

Herring salad from Norway
4 servings

4 fillets of matjes herring
3 carrots
2 onions
6 medium-sized potatoes, boiled and cold

Dressing:
2 tbsp vinegar
⅓ cup (1 dl) oil
salt
pepper

Peel and wash carrots and cut them into thin slices. Peel potatoes and slice them thin. Peel and slice onions. Cut herrings into 1″ (2.5 cm) pieces. Layer potatoes, carrots, onions and herrings in a deep dish and pour dressing over them. Chill for several hours.

By the turn of the century a classic smörgåsbord consisted of more food than anybody would want to sample. There were several varieties of herring and of smelt dishes. There were warm dishes like

Marinated herring

kidney stew, meatballs, omelets, spare ribs, tiny
hot dogs, cheeses and at least three kinds of bread.
And even so, the smörgåsbord was supposed to be
followed by at least one main course plus dessert.

Marinated herring
4 servings

4 large fillets of fresh herring

Brine:
4 cups (1 l) water
⅔ cup (1½ dl) coarse salt (kosher salt)
4 tbsp sugar

Marinade:
1⅓ cup (3½ dl) pickling vinegar
2 cups (5 dl) water
1½ cup (3½ dl) sugar
1 tbsp whole allspice
1 tsp whole pepper
½ tsp ground pepper
2 tsp dill seeds
1 tsp whole cloves
4 onions
1 leek (or 3 spring onions)

Wash fillets and drain. Boil ingredients for brine and cool. Pour brine over herring fillets and chill for 2 days. Remove fish from brine, wash and drain. Mix ingredients for marinade and boil. Cool. Put herring fillets and sliced onions and leek into a crock or deep dish and pour cold marinade over them. Fish may have to be weighted to stay in marinade. Use a small plate and a jar filled with water or a small clean rock. Marinate in refrigerator for 3 days before serving.

Dilled herring

4 fillets of salt herring
1 cup (2½ dl) finely chopped onion
4 tbsp chopped dill

Marinade:
¾ cup (2 dl) pickling vinegar
¾ cup (2 dl) water
¾ cup (2 dl) sugar
5 grains of pepper

Soak fillets in water for about 8 hours. Boil vinegar, water, sugar and pepper for marinade and cool. Cut fillets into ½″ (1 cm) pieces. Layer herring, onion and dill in a wide-mouthed jar. Cover the fish with marinade. Marinate in refrigerator for 1 day.

Today the classic smörgåsbord is found mainly in restaurants. For a fixed price you can eat as much as you dare. There are special rules for attacking it. You start with the herring and fish dishes.

Danish omelet
4 servings

A hearty breakfast dish, which combines the main products of Danish agriculture: pork, eggs and cream. It can also be served on a smörgåsbord.

6 slices of salt pork (if you can't find salt pork, bacon will do)
2 tomatoes
2 raw potatoes
6 eggs
⅓ cup (1 dl) table cream
salt
pepper
1 bunch of spring onions or chives

Fry salt pork and drain on a piece of paper towel. Peel potatoes, cut into small cubes, and fry in pork drippings for 7 minutes or till tender. Pour off excess fat. Mix potatoes together with pork and add sliced tomatoes. Beat eggs and cream with a fork, season with (salt and) pepper, and add to pan. Shake the skillet and tilt it a little, or stir with a fork, so the omelet cooks evenly. When it's done, slice spring onions thinly and sprinkle them on top. Serve straight from the skillet.

Baked omelet
4 servings

Omelet is a good breakfast or luncheon dish. For a smörgåsbord the omelet is topped with creamed mushrooms, kidney, shrimp, spinach or some other vegetable. Prepare topping after you put the batter in the oven, and pour it hot over the finished omelet.

3 eggs
1 tbsp flour
1⅔ cup (4 dl) milk
salt
pepper
butter

Preheat oven to 400°. Beat flour into milk and bring to a quick boil. Cool. Beat in eggs, one at a time. Season. Butter an ovenware skillet or low dish. Pour in batter and cook for about 30 minutes or until omelet is cooked and slightly browned.

You change plates to have meat and egg dishes and salads, then change plates once more for the cheeses. In Scandinavian homes a scaled-down version of the smörgåsbord is prepared for special occasions,

Creamed kidney

½ lb (250 g) fresh or canned mushrooms
1 lb (450 g) veal kidney
1 tbsp butter
salt
pepper
1 tbsp flour
¾ cup (2 dl) beef and mushroom stock
½ cup (1 dl) cream
2 tbsp dry sherry

Clean mushrooms and cut into thin slices
lengthwise. Soak kidneys in cold water and
vinegar, 1 tsp/quart (liter) for 1 hour.
Drain. Place in saucepan and cover with cold
water. Heat slowly to boiling point. Remove
from heat and rinse in cold water. Drain
well. Remove most of the fat and heavy veins
from kidneys and cut in slices or cubes.
Heat half of butter in skillet; add kidneys
and brown evenly. Remove to platter. Heat
remaining butter and brown mushrooms.
Return kidneys. Season. Sprinkle flour over
mixture and stir well, gradually adding
stock and cream. Simmer 10 to 15 minutes.
Add wine and season to taste. Serve in
omelet or pastry shells.

Creamed shrimp
4 servings

1 tbsp butter
3 tbsp flour
2 cups (5 dl) half and half
1½ cup (3—4 dl) cooked, chopped shrimp
salt
pepper
2 tbsp finely chopped dill

Melt butter over low heat and stir in flour.
Add half and half. Simmer and stir over low
heat until the sauce thickens. Season and
stir in shrimp.

for parties, or for visiting foreigners. A small
smörgåsbord, a buffet table with food prepared in
advance so the guests can help themselves whenever
they please, is a practical idea for entertaining.

Cattle in fertile green fields

Meat Dishes

Dilled lamb or veal

4 servings

This is a favorite Swedish stew. It should be seasoned with coarsely chopped fresh dill, but dried dill leaves out of a jar will give a similar flavor. Scandinavian lamb is a lean meat. If the lamb you buy is fat, the meat should be boiled a day ahead and cooled in the stock. The fat will rise to the surface and harden, and is easy to lift off. Otherwise you get a very fatty dish.

2½ lb (1¼ kg) lamb or veal shoulder or breast
For every 2 cups (4 dl) of water:
2 tsp salt
5 grains of pepper
1 bay leaf
1 onion
dill (use the stalks, keep the tiny leaves for
    the sauce)

Sauce:
1 tbsp butter
3 tbsp flour
2 cups (4 dl) stock
(1 egg yolk)
¼ — ½ cup (1 dl) table cream
1 — 2 tbsp lemon juice or cider vinegar
3 tbsp chopped dill

Pour cold water over the meat so that it is barely covered. Boil and skim. Now add spices, sliced onions and dill, cover and simmer until meat is tender, about 1 hour.

Melt butter and stir in flour. Stirring constantly over low heat, add 2 cups (5 dl) of strained stock and continue to cook slowly until the gravy is thickened. Add table cream to smoothen it, or 1 egg yolk diluted in a few tablespoons of cream. Season with salt, pepper and lemon juice or vinegar to taste and add chopped dill. Cut meat into bit-sized pieces (discard some of the bones) and heat in gravy. Serve with rice or boiled potatoes.

Housewives of earlier generations were often reduced to using salted raw products, when not being able to buy fresh provisions. Salting was the only preservation method in use beside smoking and drying.

Sailor's beef stew

4 servings

1 lb (500 g) lean stewing beef in bit-sized
   cubes
salt
pepper
bay leaf
2 tbsp butter
2 onions
5—6 medium-sized potatoes
1½ cup (4 dl) stock

Slice onions and brown them. Brown meat
and season well with salt and pepper. Peel
and slice raw potatoes. Butter the bottom of a
heavy pan and layer potatoes, meat, onions
and seasoning. The bottom and top layers
should be potatoes. Add stock (of beef bouillon cube) and cover. Simmer for 1—1½
hours.

For stronger flavor, try using 1 cup (2½ dl)
of stock and ½ cup (1 dl) of (Danish) beer.
But don't be too generous with the beer;
more than ½ cup (1 dl) gives the stew a
bitter flavor.

Beef stew

4—6 servings

*This is the classic Scandinavian meat stew.
It gets its particular flavor from allspice and
bay leaf and from the jelly that's added at
the very end. If you can't find red currant
jelly a tablespoon or two of cranberry jelly
will give a similar flavor.*

3 lb (1½ kg) chuck or stewing beef
salt
pepper
2—3 tbsp flour
2 tbsp butter
3 onions
2 bay leaves
4 whole grains of allspice
2 cups (5 dl) stock
(¼ cup (½ dl) table cream)
red currant jelly to season the gravy

Cut meat into bit-sized pieces, season with
salt and pepper and roll in flour. Slice onions.
Sauté meat and onions, add bay leaves and
coarsely crushed allspice. Add stock, cover
and simmer for 1½ hours or until meat is
tender. Season gravy with 1—2 tbsp red
currant jelly. It should have a strong, slightly
sweet and sour taste. If the gravy is too thin,
thicken with 1 tbsp flour or cornstarch in a
few tablespoons of cream or milk. Serve with
boiled potatoes and currant jelly or lingonberries (cranberry sauce or jelly).

Salting demanded a great culinary skill by the Scandinavian housewives to be able to create delicious
dishes from such poor products. The best they could
do was to season the food heavily and add potatoes

Beef with horse-radish

4 servings

This is a classic Scandinavian way of preparing inexpensive cuts of beef; they are boiled with vegetables and spices which enhance the taste of the meat.

2—2½ lb (1 kg) chuck or brisket of beef
For every quart (liter) water:
1 carrot
1 small parsnip
1 small piece celery root
1 chopped onion
1 tbsp salt
5 whole allspice
1 bay leaf

Sauce:
1½ tbsp butter
2 tbsp flour
1 cup (2½ dl) beef stock
1 cup (2½ dl) milk
salt
pepper
2—3 tbsp grated horse-radish

Place meat in kettle and barely cover with water. Bring to boiling point and skim. Add vegetables, bring to boiling point and skim. Add salt, allspice and bay leaf and simmer for about 2 hours or until meat is tender.

Melt butter in saucepan. Add flour and stir until well blended. Gradually stir in stock and milk. Simmer 5 minutes, stirring occasionally. Season. Add grated horse-radish. Don't boil sauce after adding horse-radish or flavor will be bitter.

and different root vegetables. Cooking to these earlier generations of housewives was of course very time consuming. For the big feasts, which were very common in these days, one had to start the

Rolled steaks
4 servings

*A good, spicy, old-fashioned beef casserole
which used to be served as a Sunday dinner.
It's not as complicated as it may sound;
to roll and secure the meat is not difficult,
and if a roll or two comes undone, the
gravy will taste even better for it. The rolled
steaks are served with potatoes and pickled
cucumber, see page 38.*

1 lb (500 g) sandwich steaks, thin slices of
   top round (or other thin slices of beef)
1 small piece fat back
2 sour pickles
twigs of parsley
2 onions
2 carrots
1 celery stalk
1 bay leaf
a pinch of thyme
a pinch of allspice
2—3 tbsp butter
1 tbsp flour
1 cup (2½ dl) table cream
2 tsp tomato purée
1 cup (2½ dl) stock

Cut meat into pieces about the size of your
hand—large enough to be filled and rolled,
small enough to make one serving each.
Cut fat back into thin strips. Season them
with salt, pepper and allspice. Cut pickles
into strips, chop onions and carrots coarsely.

Put 1—2 strips of seasoned fat back, 1 strip
of pickle, about 1 tsp onion and 1 tsp carrot
on each piece of meat. Roll meat and secure
with toothpicks.

Brown meat carefully in a frying pan, using
about 1½ tbsp butter. Sauté onions and
carrots in remaining butter in a heavy pot
with a well fitted lid. Dust with flour, stir in
stock and continue stirring until sauce has
thickened. Season with thyme and tomato
purée. Put meat rolls into gravy and simmer
very gently (they'll come undone otherwise),
until they are tender, 15—40 minutes, depending on the quality of the meat. (You can
pour a few tablespoons of water into the
frying pan, heat it, and add this to the meat
in the pot.) When the meat is tender, add
about ½ cup (1 dl) cream, heat, correct
seasoning and serve.

preparations at least one week ahead. For today's
housewives it is much easier. One uses to a great
extent semi-manufactured products from the food
industry. Many of the dishes that you'll find in

Roast leg of elk

Northern Scandinavia has an abundance of
elk. The meat is sold fresh in the fall,
frozen the rest of the year. There is elk or
moose in the northern United States, but
most states prohibit the sale of game. To
taste elk meat in the U.S. you have to hunt
yourself or know somebody who does.

Elk has dark meat with a strong gamy taste,
stronger than deer. Cuts from young animals
can be larded and roasted. Older animals are
tougher and the meat is best if it is marinated
for a day or two before it is braised. Any
marinade for venison can be used. Scandinavians usually add crushed juniper
berries to the marinade. Roast the meat,
following any recipe for venison. In Scandinavia elk is served with potatoes and with
lingonberries or crab apple or mountain ash
jelly. The small red berries from mountain
ash make a bitter, clear orange jelly. Any cut
of elk, not just the leg, should be treated as
venison. Ground elk meat can be mixed with
ground pork. Elk has lean meat; the pork-
elk mixture gives juicy and very tasty meatballs and an excellent dark gravy.

Karelian stew
6 servings

*A very simple, hearty stew that gets its
flavor from the mixture of various meats.
It takes 2 hours to cook, but takes care of
itself during most of that time.*

1 lb (500 g) chuck
1 lb (500 g) veal (shoulder or breast)
**1 lb (500 g) lean pork (picnic shoulder or
    shoulder butt)**
1—2 tbsp salt
coarsely ground pepper
2 bay leaves
2 onions
hot water

Preheat oven to 375°. Cut meat into bit-sized
pieces, season well and arrange in a deep
ovenware dish or pot. Put the fat pieces
on top. Add sliced onions. Add hot water so
that it barely covers the meat. Cover and
cook for about 2 hours. Remove lid for the
last half hour of cooking. Some of the water
should be reduced, making a nice gravy and
the meat on top should be slightly browned.

this chapter about meat can be bought in the Scandinavian food markets as semi-manufactured products.
Many dishes are finished products in cans and many
others you can find deep frozen or as dryed products.

Marinated pot roast

6 servings

This preparation is reminiscent of the German Sauerbraten. Once upon a time marinades were used to make tough meat tender and to preserve it. Today the marinade is used to add flavor. It's not much trouble — you mix a marinade and leave the roast in it from a night to several days; the juicy and flavorful meat is well worth the extra labor.

4—5 lb (2—2½ kg) chuck roast

Marinade:
1 cup (2½ dl) light beer
⅓ cup (1 dl) vinegar
1 tbsp crushed pepper
2 tsp crushed allspice
3 crushed bay leaves
2 tsp thyme
2 sliced onions
2 sliced carrots

To roast:
2 tbsp butter
1 cup (2½ dl) marinade
salt
pepper

Mix ingredients for the marinade. Put the meat into a bowl and add marinade. The marinade should cover the meat. Cover the bowl with foil and refrigerate for 1—4 days.

Turn the meat from time to time. Remove meat from marinade and dry it with a paper towel. Rub it with salt and pepper. Strain and reserve marinade.

Use a heavy pot with a well fitted lid. Heat butter and brown meat on all sides. Add marinade and turn down heat. Cover the pot and simmer slowly until the meat is done, which can take anywhere from 1½—3 hours, depending on the tenderness of the meat, how long it has been marinating and how thick the piece is. The heat should be quite low. If too much marinade evaporates, add a little water.

Remove roast and keep it hot on a platter. Thicken the gravy with 1—2 tsp cornstarch: dissolve cornstarch in cold water and gradually add to the boiling gravy in the pot. Stir and let boil, then remove from heat. Now add a few tablespoons to ½ cup (1 dl) cream. Check seasoning, add salt, pepper or a little bit of ground allspice. The gravy should be thick and plentiful and have a strong taste. Pot roast is traditionally served with sour gherkins and lingonberry jelly (or cranberry sauce) and with steaming boiled potatoes.

However, it doesn't matter how well the food industry has succeeded in making these products, there is no doubt that the home-cooked food, where one has used genuine raw products, has the very best

Braised goose
8 servings

1 goose of 10—12 lb (5 kg)
1 lemon
salt
pepper
2 cups (4—5 dl) good chicken stock

Stuffing:
tart apples
pitted prunes

Gravy:
degreased juices from the goose, plus stock
    to make about 2 cups (4—5 dl) liquid
1 tbsp cornstarch
2 tbsp brandy
(soy sauce)
(red currant jelly)

Preheat oven to 300—350°. Season goose
with salt and pepper and rub inside and out
with lemon. Pare and quarter tart apples and
stuff goose with a mixture of apples and
pitted prunes. Secure the opening with small
skewers and a criss-crossed string, and tie
the ends of the drumsticks together so the
legs will be close to the body. Place on a rack
in a roasting pan and pour stock into pan.
Roast for approximately 4 hours or until
done. (Figure 20—25 minutes to the pound.)
Leave oven door slightly ajar for the last
10 minutes of cooking.

Carefully pour off all the drippings before
goose is completely done. Degrease as much
as possible. Thicken with cornstarch in a few
tablespoons of cold water or stock. Season
well with salt, pepper, brandy, a teaspoon of
soy sauce or a little bit of red currant jelly.
Braised goose is served with boiled or fried
potatoes, spicy red cabbage (see page 108),
stewed prunes (they can be simmered in a
little bit of wine), stewed apple halves or
apple sauce and red currant jelly.

taste and the most nutritive value. It is possible
that you will find many of these dishes too rich
and too heavy. The calorie intake is generally also
somewhat higher in the Scandinavian countries.

Boiled cured duckling
4 servings

This recipe dates back to the middle ages when curing of meat and fowl was far more common than it is today. It was done partly to preserve food, partly to balance an excessively fat diet. A cured duckling is very tender. The salty taste makes the fat meat more enjoyable and probably easier to digest.

one 5 lb (2 kg) duckling
1 lemon
1 cup (2 dl) salt
½ cup (1 dl) sugar

Brine:
for every cup (2½ dl) of water, use
3 tbsp salt and 1 tbsp sugar

Stock for boiling:
water
1 carrot
1 onion
3 grains of pepper
1 bay leaf
parsley

Rub duckling inside and out with lemon, salt and sugar. Chill for 12 hours. Boil ingredients for brine (you'll need about 6 cups) (1½ l) and cool. Pour cold brine over the duckling and store weighted and covered in refrigerator for 2 days.

Drain the duckling and fasten legs so they will be close to the body by tying the ends of the drumsticks together. Put in enough cold water to cover. Boil and skim, then add sliced carrot, onion and spices and simmer until tender, about 1½ hours. Cured duckling is served warm with potatoes, apple sauce and vegetables, or cold with whipped cream seasoned with horse-radish. If the whipped cream sounds too outlandish, you can use any prepared horse-radish sauce.

Probably, it can maybe be related to the climate conditions. As you know it is considerably cooler in Scandinavia than in England and in greater parts of North America. We therefore would like to suggest

Danish meat patties

6 servings

1½ lb (700 g) ground lean pork
1 finely chopped onion
salt
pepper
dash of allspice
3 eggs
3—4 tbsp flour
1½ cup (3½ dl) table cream
butter
1½ cup (3½ dl) stock (made from bouillon
   cube and water)
1—2 tsp soy sauce

Stir eggs with flour and 1 cup (2½ dl) of
cream. Work this mixture into ground meat
together with chopped onions and spices.
Let rest for about half an hour. The mixture
should be firm enough so that you can make
patties. If it is too firm you can add a little
water.

Make thin patties about the size of your palm
and fry them in hot butter, a few minutes on
each side. They should be well done. Remove
them. Stir remaining cream and stock into
the frying pan. Season with soy sauce. Strain
the gravy. Serve the meat patties with gravy
and boiled potatoes. Buttered spinach is
often served together with them.

Swedish hamburger

4 servings

1 lb (450 g) ground beef
2 boiled potatoes
1 egg
1 cup (2 dl) milk
salt
pepper
½ cup (1 dl) chopped pickled beets
2 tbsp chopped onion
2 tbsp chopped capers
butter

Peel boiled potatoes and mash them with
a fork. Mix into ground meat together with
egg and seasoning. Add beets, onion and
capers and stir well. Make hamburger patties
and fry in butter or broil to taste. Swedish
hamburgers are sometimes served topped
with a fried egg.

that some of these dishes are served with only a
salad instead of the gravy and potatoes, if you think
the meal will be too heavy for you. These dishes
should be considered as "real dinners".

Meat Loaf
4 servings

Prepare Meatball mixture, see page 6 (onions can be omitted), mixing in an additional ¾ cup (2 dl) milk or water
2 onions
2 tbsp butter
4 medium-sized tomatoes
½ cup (1 dl) grated cheese

Preheat oven to 375°. Peel and slice onions and sauté slowly in butter until almost tender. Butter a baking dish and layer meat and onions, topping with meat mixture. Cover top with sliced tomatoes and sprinkle with grated cheese. Bake for approximately 50 minutes. Cover with foil if top gets brown before meat is done. Hot meat loaf is usually served with potatoes and a salad. It's delicious cold and sliced for sandwiches.

Danish curried meatballs
6 servings

1½ lb (700 g) ground lean pork (see page 6)
1 onion
salt, pepper
1⅓ cup (3 dl) half and half
3 eggs
3 tbsp flour
4—6 cups (1½ l) stock made of bouillon cube and water

Curry sauce:
1 chopped onion
1 tart apple, chopped
3 tbsp butter
2 tbsp curry
3 tbsp flour
2 cups (5 dl) stock (use the stock in which the meatballs were cooked)
1 cup (2 dl) half and half
salt, pepper

Chop onion and mix into ground meat. Beat eggs together with flour and half and half, season with salt and pepper and mix into ground meat. Heat stock. Roll small meatballs and simmer in stock, 7—8 minutes.

Sauté chopped onion and apple in butter. Add curry and sauté for a few minutes. Stir in flour and, when well blended, add stock and half and half. Stir over low heat until well combined and thickened. Season to taste and heat meatballs in sauce. Serve with boiled rice.

This means that they are served as the main meal of the day, often already at noon or at one o'clock p.m. Lamb and pork are popular kinds of meat in Scandinavia. Lamb is easy to breed in Scandinavia.

Farmer's omelet

4 servings

2 onions
2 tbsp butter
4 boiled potatoes
4 frankfurters
4 eggs
4 tbsp water
salt
3 tbsp finely chopped parsley

Chop onions and sauté in skillet. Add cubed potatoes and franks and brown. Beat eggs and water with a fork, season and pour into skillet. Tilt the skillet and stick the omelet with a fork so that it cooks evenly. Sprinkle parsley over the cooked omelet and serve from skillet.

Liver hash from Finland

4 servings

The liver for this old-fashioned recipe has to be ground. You can grind it yourself in a meat grinder, or put it through a blender.

1 lb (500 g) baby beef liver
5 cups (1¼ l) milk
1 cup (2½ dl) rice (choose a variety with round, short kernels, not the long Carolina rice)
1 onion
2 tbsp butter
3—4 tbsp syrup
⅔ cup (1½ dl) raisins
salt
pepper
marjoram

Pour rice into the cold milk, heat slowly and simmer until the rice is soft, about 25 minutes. Let the mixture cool. Preheat oven to 375°. Chop onion and fry in butter until it is transparent but not browned. Mix liver, syrup, raisins and onion into the rice. Season with salt, pepper and marjoram. Cook the rice and liver mixture in a buttered dish for about 1 hour. Serve with cranberry jelly and melted butter.

It is an animal which doesn't require too much pasture but likes bushy meadows. No soil is too meagre and no land too wooded for raising sheep. Lamb meat is tender, juicy and easily digested.

Beef steak

Lamb meat is good for boiling. It is often cooked
with cabbage, onions, carrots and potatoes. These
are the most common root vegetables in Scandinavia.
Among the recipes there are two very typical Fin-

28

Beef steak

Scandinavians like their steaks thin and medium to well done. Use sandwich steaks or top round, if it is tender, and pan fry in butter. The Scandinavian steak is always served with heaps of fried onions. Use one medium-sized onion per steak. Slice thinly and sauté till brown and tender. Keep hot while frying the meat and top each slice with a generous heaping of fried onions. The drippings are sometimes mixed with a little stock and poured over the meat. Potatoes are served with the meat, which is eaten with mustard.

Scandinavian hash
4 servings

A well made Scandinavian hash is a treat — in spite of the fact that it's made of left-overs. Probably it was invented by a thrifty housewife; today it's served even in first class restaurants. The hash is supposed to be well browned, and not mushy. To achieve this, onions and potatoes have to be browned separately. The more varieties of left-over meat you mix into it, the better it tastes. The American housewife could mix in sausage meat, which should be cooked apart so that the hash doesn't get too greasy. If you take care to cube the potatoes neatly, the hash will also look good. Often the hash is served with a fried egg or a raw egg yolk per person and pickled beets.

2 onions
2—3 tbsp butter
6—8 boiled, cold potatoes
1½ cup (3—4 dl) cooked left-over meat
    (roast beef, pork roast, pork chops, leg of
    lamb, ham)
salt
pepper
chopped parsley for garnish

Chop onions. Cube potatoes and left-over meat. Sauté onions until nicely browned. Remove from skillet. Sauté potato cubes. Mix in meat and reheat onions, season well with salt and pepper and garnish with chopped parsley.

nish dishes made of lamb; lamb and cabbage stew and lamb stew from Finland. Even if these dishes originated in Finland, they are also common in Sweden and Norway. In Denmark they have for a long

Piroshki

Piroshki can be made with flaky pastry (see page 90) or pie dough.

**Flaky pastry or pie dough made from
   2½ cups (6 dl) flour**

Filling I:
¾ cup (2 dl) rice
2 cups (5 dl) stock
2 tbsp butter
1 onion
2 cups (5 dl) cooked left-over meat
1 cup (2½ dl) stock
4 hard-boiled eggs
salt
pepper
1 egg

Boil stock and slowly stir in rice. Do not cover. Boil vigorously for 20 minutes. Pour into a colander. Rinse rice with cold water and drain well. Chop onion and sauté in butter. Add cubed meat, stir in stock and season well. Add rice and mix in chopped eggs. Season well.

Filling II:
1 large cabbage
3 tbsp butter
1—2 cups (3—5 dl) stock
salt
pepper
1—2 tbsp syrup

Shred cabbage and parboil in salted water for 5 minutes. Drain well. Brown in butter, add stock and simmer until tender. Season with salt, pepper and syrup to taste. Cabbage should be moist but not wet. Drain off excess liquid, which otherwise will run over the edges of the pie.

It's difficult to roll out a large piece of pie dough or flaky pastry to an even square. If you aren't a skilled baker, make two smaller piroshki instead of a single large one. Roll out a little less than ¼ of the dough into a square about ⅛—¼" (½ cm) thick. How thick the pastry should be is a matter of taste and skill. Spread half of either filling to within about 1" (3 cm) of edges. Roll out another fourth of the dough and place on top. Moisten the edges and pinch down with a fork. Cut a small vent in the middle, or prick with a fork to allow the steam to escape; otherwise you may get a soggy crust.

Beat egg, add 1 tbsp of water, and brush onto the surface of the dough. For a pie dough: preheat oven to 450°. Bake piroshki for 10 minutes, then reduce heat to 350°. Bake until done, approximately 30 minutes. If the pastry colors too rapidly, cover with foil.

time been experts on breeding pigs. Today they are striving towards getting them as lean as possible. The Danes like rich food and they have many succulent pork dishes such as for example stewed hocks

Stuffed cabbage

6 servings

1 head of cabbage, about 3 lb (1—1½ kg)
water
salt

Stuffing:
4 tbsp rice
½ cup (1 dl) water
¾—1 cup (2 dl) milk
¾ lb (300 g) ground meat, preferably ground
   beef and ground lean pork mixed
salt
pepper
½ cup (1 dl) milk
butter
2 tbsp syrup
¾ cup (2 dl) hot stock
(1 tsp cumin)

Trim stem and outer, damaged leaves from a head of cabbage and boil 5—10 minutes: you'll need approximately 2 quarts (2 l) of water. Drain and cool so that cabbage can be handled, then carefully peel off leaves. Prepare stuffing: wash rice and pour into boiling water. Cook till water is almost evaporated, then add milk, cover, and simmer over low heat until rice is very tender. Cool.

Preheat oven to 375°. Mix rice and meat, add a little more milk to a soft mixture and season well with salt and pepper. Put about 1 tbsp of stuffing in the middle of each cabbage leaf and roll tightly, tucking in the edges. Place them close together in a buttered baking dish. Dot each roll with a little butter (and some cumin) and syrup. Pour stock into dish and bake till cabbage is brown and very tender, about 45 minutes.

Remove cabbage rolls to a serving dish and keep them hot. Add some more stock if there is too little left at the bottom of the baking dish, and season well. Cream can be added. For a thick gravy, melt 1 tbsp butter, stir in 2 tbsp flour and add stock (and soy sauce), stirring constantly over low heat until sauce has thickened. Season well and pour over cabbage, or heat stuffed cabbage very carefully in the gravy. Stuffed cabbage is usually served with boiled potatoes or rice and lingonberries. Cranberry sauce will also do well. For variety the cabbage rolls can be cooked with thin strips of bacon. Roll a strip of bacon around each cabbage roll before putting it into the baking dish. Don't add any additional salt. Cook and serve according to above recipe.

with cabbage. The price for pork is in comparison with other meats low and large amounts of pork are consumed in Scandinavia. Beef is expensive in Scandinavia, which is the case in most parts of the

Cabbage pudding

4 servings

1 medium-sized cabbage
butter or shortening
salt
pepper
bay leaf

Stuffing:
see Stuffed cabbage, page 31

Preheat oven to 400°. Trim off stem and outer, damaged leaves of cabbage. Quarter, then shred cabbage and sauté covered over low heat for approximately 15 minutes. Season well with salt, pepper and bay leaf. Prepare stuffing according to recipe for Stuffed cabbage, page 31. Butter a baking dish. Cover with a layer of cabbage. Spread stuffing and top with the remaining cabbage. Dot with butter and bake for about 1 hour or until the meat is cooked and the cabbage nicely browned. Serve with boiled potatoes and lingonberries or cranberry sauce or jelly.

Lamb and cabbage stew

4 servings

2 lb (1 kg) lean lamb shoulder or breast
1 medium-sized cabbage
(3 tbsp butter)
salt
10 grains of pepper
2 bay leaves
1—2 cups (3—4 dl) water
chopped parsley

Shred cabbage and cut meat into bit-sized pieces. Brown in butter, season with salt, pepper and bay leaves and add water so that the mixture is barely covered. Cover and simmer until meat is tender, about 1½ hours. Check seasoning, sprinkle with parsley and serve with boiled potatoes.

world today. Because of the high price for beef meat, things are added to make the dish go further in many of the recipes you'll find here. One has chosen to make beef stews or ground beef so it will

Stewed hocks with cabbage
6 servings

This is a simple, inexpensive and very rich meal to serve on a chilly day. It takes 2—2½ hours to prepare, but once it's stewing in the pot it needs little or no supervision.

1 large head of cabbage
2 large onions
4 slices of salt pork
(butter or lard)
4 cloves
¼—½ cup (½—1 dl) brown sugar
2 tbsp cider vinegar
salt
pepper
2 small pork hocks
2—4 cups (½—1 l) water

Trim stalk and discard outer leaves of cabbage, then shred it finely. Sauté salt pork over low heat in large pot. Remove pork slices and sauté shredded cabbage in drippings. Add 1—2 tbsp butter or lard if there aren't enough drippings. Peel onions, stick cloves in them and add to cabbage. Stir over low heat until it is evenly browned. Sprinkle with salt, sugar, pepper and add vinegar and water. Add pork hocks and slices of salt pork, cover and simmer till meat is done, 1½—2 hours. Peeled potatoes can be added to the pork hocks for the last half hour of cooking.

Pancakes with bacon
4 servings

1½ cup (3½ dl) milk
2 eggs
⅓ cup (1 dl) flour
½ lb (250 g) bacon or salt pork

Beat eggs and milk and stir into flour to make an even batter. If you use bacon, sauté slices slowly until they are crisp. Drain them on paper towel and crumble them. Pour off the bacon fat and use it for frying pancakes. If you use salt pork, cube the piece before frying, or cut the slices into smaller pieces.

Heat a skillet, using about 1 tsp bacon fat for each pancake, and 1—2 tbsp fried bacon or salt pork. Pour a thin layer of batter, tip the skillet and let it spread evenly over the bottom. Cook the pancake over moderate heat. When it is brown, turn it and brown the other side. The smaller the skillet, the easier the pancakes are to cook and turn. Serve with cranberry sauce or jelly for a rich breakfast dish.

be enough for many portions. In earlier days the traditional veal roast used to be served for Sunday dinners in most homes. Nowadays veal roast has almost vanished from the Scandinavian tables. It has

Lamb stew from Finland
4 servings

2 lb (1 kg) lamb shoulder or breast
8 medium-sized potatoes
2 carrots
1 bunch of spring onions
salt
pepper
thyme
2 cups (5 dl) water
chopped parsley

Cut meat into bit-sized pieces. Peel and slice
potatoes and carrots. Peel and slice onions.
Layer vegetables and meat in a pot, season
with salt, pepper and thyme and pour in
enough water so that the meat is barely
covered. Cover and simmer until meat is
tender, about 1 hour. Check seasoning and
serve sprinkled with chopped parsley.

Potatoes à la Hasselbacken
4 servings

These baked potatoes are easy to prepare,
but very good and quite unusual. In Sweden,
where the dish originated, it's often served
as a party variation of the dinner potato.

8—10 medium-sized potatoes
salt
3 tbsp butter
4—5 tbsp grated cheese
unseasoned bread crumbs

Preheat oven to 450°. Peel potatoes and slice,
but not all the way through, so that the
bottom still is one piece. The easiest way of
doing this is to put one potato at a time on
a large spoon. Slice; the concave spoon keeps
the knife from cutting all the way through
the potato. Put them into a buttered baking
dish. Melt remaining butter and brush on
potatoes, sprinkle with salt, bread crumbs
and grated cheese. Bake until done, about
1 hour. Serve from baking dish.

become an expensive luxury. The European kind of
veal is hard to find in the United States too, outside
of gourmet specialty stores. Instead, something
called calf has come on the market. It is young

Potato dumplings

4 servings

Potato dumplings cannot be made from an American baking potato like an Idaho. The dough won't keep its shape and dissolves in the water. Any other kind of mature potato will do fine. If you're hesitant, make a small amount of dough and test-boil.

8 medium-sized potatoes
¾ cup (1¾ dl) flour
1 egg
½ lb (250 g) bacon or Canadian bacon
1 onion
salt
pepper
allspice
butter

Peel and boil potatoes and mash them. Cool. Mix in egg and flour to make a soft dough. Season with salt and pepper. Chop onion and sauté in butter. Cube Canadian bacon and sauté. If you use ordinary bacon, fry in slices until it is crisp. Drain and break into pieces. Mix onion and bacon and season with allspice. Roll dough into 2″ (5 cm) wide roll, cut into 2″ (5 cm) long pieces. Put about 1 tbsp of onion and bacon mixture into the center of each piece and form them into balls. Drop balls into gently boiling salted water and boil for 10—15 minutes. Drain them well. Serve with melted butter or lingonberries (cranberry sauce).

Swedish potato pancakes

4 servings

8 medium-sized potatoes
2 eggs
1 tsp salt
butter or lard to fry them in

Peel potatoes and grate them coarsely. Mix with 2 eggs and salt. Fry pancakes, the size of an ordinary pancake (about 4″ (10 cm) in diameter). Serve potato pancakes with bacon and lingonberries or cranberry sauce (or syrup if you prefer to eat them American fashion).

beef cattle which has not yet been corn-fed, and which is less tender than corn-fed beef. A calf roast may be good—but it is a far cry from the traditional Scandinavian veal roast, which was

Creamed potatoes
4 servings

These potatoes are good with bacon, salt pork or sausage; very often they are served together with smoked fish.

2 tbsp butter
2 tbsp flour
1¾ cup (4 dl) milk
salt
pepper
dash of nutmeg
4 tbsp chopped parsley
6—8 boiled potatoes

Melt butter over low heat and stir in flour. Add milk stirring constantly until sauce thickens and continue simmering for 4—5 minutes. Season with salt, freshly ground pepper and a dash of nutmeg. Add cubed boiled potatoes and heat. Serve sprinkled with parsley.

Variation
Creamed potatoes can be made from raw cubed potatoes. Combine butter, seasoning, 6 cubed raw potatoes, and 1½ cup (3½ dl) heavy cream in a double boiler, cover and simmer very slowly until potatoes are tender and sauce has thickened. Garnish-season with chopped dill. This variation has a finer taste, but is also more complicated and more expensive to make.

Brown beans
4 servings

Scandinavian brown beans, available only in Scandinavian grocery stores, are close to kidney beans, which can be used for this recipe.

1¾ cup (4 dl) Scandinavian brown beans
4 cups (1 l) water
½ tbsp salt
4 tbsp syrup or brown sugar
1—3 tbsp vinegar

Wash and soak beans over night in salted water. Boil in the same water until tender, 1—1½ hours. Stir from time to time and add more water if necessary. Season with brown sugar, vinegar and salt. The beans should be mild, and slightly sweet and sour. Brown beans are served with fried salt pork or with meatballs and are a traditional Scandinavian dish.

taken from milk-fed animals with a light-pink and very tender meat. A simple and liked form of invitation in Scandinavia is to invite to a Dutch treat party. One is then able to invite many guests with-

Mashed potatoes-rutabaga

4 servings

1 rutabaga, about 1 lb (500 g)
4—6 medium-sized potatoes
3—4 cups (¾—1 l) stock
(salt)
5 grains of pepper
5 grains of allspice

Peel rutabaga and slice. Put into boiling stock together with coarsely crushed pepper and allspice. Depending on the saltiness of the stock, you may have to add salt. Cook for 20 minutes. Now add peeled and sliced potatoes, cover, and continue boiling until rutabaga and potatoes are very tender. Drain and reserve stock. Put vegetables through a blender; add stock a little at a time until the mixture has the consistency of fluffy mashed potatoes. A piece of butter can be stirred in to enhance the taste. Serve with corned beef, sausage or cured ham.

Braised rutabagas

4 servings

Rutabagas are a traditional Scandinavian vegetable, so much that in some parts of the U.S they are even called Swedes. Some people love them, others wouldn't touch them. They have a strong, very special taste that's something like cabbage. Before potatoes were imported from America to Europe, rutabagas were the mainstay of the Scandinavian diet. They are still in-expensive, and are associated with down-to-earth country food. Try them together with corned beef, or with hot sausage, cured ham, or salt pork.

If you've never tasted rutabagas, maybe you should start with Mashed potatoes—rutabaga (see recipe beside), a fluffy orange-colored mash which is a mixture of rutabagas and potatoes. In Mashed potatoes—rutabaga the flavor of rutabagas is not as startling to the uninitiated as when they are served alone.

1 large rutabaga
2—3 tbsp butter
½ cup (1 dl) stock
salt

Peel rutabaga and cube. Sauté slowly in butter. Add stock, cover and simmer until tender. Check seasoning; they may need a bit more salt. Serve with an extra tablespoon of butter.

out too high costs. The guests bring their specialities and the host serves bread and boiled potatoes and wine or beer. To a Dutch treat party the guests bring warm or cold dishes in suitable bowls.

Pickled cucumber

This old-fashioned cucumber salad used to be served with the traditional veal roast for Sunday dinner. Fortunately the pickled cucumber salad is good with Rolled steaks (see page 20) and with any cold meat, with ham, meatballs and even hamburgers.

6 cucumbers, about 3 lb (1½ kg)
3 tbsp dill seeds
1⅔ cup (4 dl) sugar
4 tbsp salt
2 tbsp mustard seeds
1¼ cup (3 dl) pickling vinegar
2 cups (5 dl) water

Mix sugar, salt, mustard seeds, vinegar and water, and stir until sugar is completely dissolved. Wash cucumbers and slice thinly. Layer cucumber slices with dill seeds in wide-mouthed jars, pour the vinegar mixture over them and cover with foil. Store in re-frigerator. Will keep 2—3 weeks.

Danish sauerkraut
4—6 servings

1 can (1 lb) (450 g) sauerkraut
2 onions
4 whole cloves
1 tsp coarsely crushed caraway
(3—4 tbsp water or white wine)

Strain sauerkraut and rinse it with cold water. Chop 2 onions. Simmer sauerkraut for about 30 minutes together with onions and spices. Keep the sauerkraut covered. If it looks dry, add a little water or a few tablespoons white wine.

In Denmark this sauerkraut is often served with "kassler", smoked pork loin, which has been cooked separately. You can add 1 smoked pork chop per person and simmer them with the sauerkraut. They should be done within 15 minutes. Serve with boiled potatoes and mustard.

Finnish liver, meatballs in curry sauce, sailor's beef, potato dumplings stuffed with chopped pork, different kinds of marinated herring dishes are excellent dishes to bring to a Dutch treat party.

Vegetables

Fresh vegetables used to be a big treat. As long as Scandinavians had to rely on what their own countries produced, the first sweet peas, the very first spinach, the first beets of the year were something to look forward to and enjoy the way an American suburbanite enjoys his first home-grown corn or his very own tomatoes. Today almost any vegetable is available all year round. Still, the first tomatoes and the first Scandinavian strawberries have kept some of their mystique. Usually the home-grown varieties are far more expensive than the imported ones. Tender sweet peas, beets, small carrots or (white) asparagus will be served as a vegetable dish at the start of a meal or after the main course and eaten only with butter, maybe with a few drops of lemon added to it. Try fresh beets the Scandinavian way: boil them in salted water (do not overcook), quickly peel off the skin, slice them and add a generous amount of butter. They're delicious, even if they grew in California!

Dill
is the herb that dominates Scandinavian cooking. It has a cool, tangy flavor, a subtle but inimitable perfume. It is best when fresh.

Larger grocery stores may carry it. It's also easy to grow and the tall plant (2—3 feet) with its light green feathery leaves is pretty to look at. A few stalks will suffice for an entire summer's worth of Scandinavian dishes. Both the leaves and the seeds, used for cooking lobster and crayfish, can be dried at home. Dried dill leaves and seeds are available at most grocery stores.

Parsley
is used extensively in Scandinavian cooking, more for looks than for taste. In Scandinavia nothing grows for many months out of the year. That's why Scandinavians cherish potted plants. Every home has them on the window sill. The abundance of parsley on the table serves much the same purpose: it's a consolation for the long winter. There is a sprig of parsley in the butter dish, on the slice of paté, on the cold cuts. Chopped parsley is heaped on fried potatoes, on vegetables, on omelets, on fish and meat dishes. It looks pretty and appetizing, and in the process Scandinavians get a much needed dose of vitamins too.

The Scandinavian main dinner course is usually accompanied by plain boiled potatoes. The fresh early summer potatoes are boiled and served with fresh dill sprigs or parsley and considered a delicacy.

Fishing boats of the west coast

Fish Dishes

Grilled eel
4 servings

This is a very old recipe from southern Sweden, easily prepared on any outdoor grill, preferably the covered kind which gives the eel a slightly smoky flavor.

1 eel of 2—3 lb (1—1½ kg)
salt (preferably coarse, kosher salt)

Clean eel but do not skin. Rub with salt and refrigerate for 6—8 hours. Heat coals in an outdoor grill. When they're red hot they should be covered with finely cut juniper branches. Juniper may be hard to come by. Cedar, which is a more common tree in the U.S will probably give some of the same smoky, woodsy flavor. You may also try chopped hemlock, which is a common tree. Wash eel, dry it with a paper towel and put it on the grill. Cook until it is dark-brown all around. Serve hot with slices of lemon and buttered baked potatoes. The meat is white, tender and delicious, the smoked-grilled fish a gourmet's treat.

Smoked eel

If you'd like to try smoked eel, but can't find it at a store, it's easy and fun to smoke the fish yourself. Pick large eels—the larger the better. Clean them but don't skin them. For smoking, any old metal can like a clean garbage can or an old oil drum will do. Put a few holes in the bottom of the can, turn it upside down, and hang the eels inside, fastening them with wire or rope. Light a charcoal fire, put a few bricks around it, and set the metal can on the bricks. Put wet branches on the coal. In Scandinavia, juniper branches are often used to add flavor to the fish. Keep the fire going but keep smothering it with wet branches: the fish needs smoke and heat.

Eel which is about 2″ (5 cm) in diameter should take 3 hours to smoke. When the fish is ready it's golden colored on the outside and the meat is a snowy white. Have ready several handfuls of salt, preferably coarse (kosher) salt. Pack the warm fish in salt and leave it till the following day.

To serve: scrape off salt, cut into bit-sized pieces, and enjoy. Smoked eel is often served with very soft scrambled eggs and with buttered spinach.

In the United States eel is often cut up for bait —a sinful waste to most Scandinavians. Eel-lovers would much rather eat the bait than for example the bluefish or anything else one could catch with eel.

Grilled pike

This is a wonderful way of preparing fish. Possibly it's an ancient method, dating from a time when food was prepared over an open fire. If you fish yourself, it's the ideal way of preparing your catch. Bass and other small fish are also delicious.

The fish must be really fresh. Clean and wash it. It doesn't have to be scaled. Have ready a mixture of chopped onion, parsley, dill, thyme, about 1 tsp of crumbled bay leaf, salt and pepper and fill it into the stomach of your fish. Secure the opening with skewers, toothpicks or strong yarn. Rub fish all around with salt and pepper.

Butter a large piece of foil and wrap it around the stuffed fish. Wrap it into layers upon layers of moist newspaper. Put it into hot coals, or into the hot ashes from an open fire. Leave fish of about 3 lb (1½ kg) for 45 minutes. Smaller fish will be done in 20 minutes. The paper is charred, the fish inside wonderfully fragrant and juicy. Serve with potatoes, baked on the same fire. The fish can also be cooked in the hot ashes from large logs in your fire place.

Broiled smelt
4 servings

2 lb (1 kg) smelt
2 tbsp salt

Herb butter:
2 oz (60 g) butter
4 tbsp finely chopped parsley and dill
1 tbsp lemon juice
salt
pepper

Wash and drain (thawed) smelt and season with salt. Broil over coal fire or a grill. The fish is supposed to be dark brown to almost black on both sides. Serve immediately — it's best when it's really hot. Herb butter and baked potatoes are served with it.

Work butter until soft and mix in other ingredients. Chill before serving.

Eel has a white, tender meat. It tastes a little like white fish, though it is not fishy at all. Served broiled or smoked it's a true gourmet treat. Southern Sweden has an eel feast late in the fall.

Stuffed smelt fillets

4 servings

Fried stuffed smelt is usually served with mashed potatoes. The stuffed smelt is excellent cold, and is often served as a snack on crisp bread together with mayonnaise. Leftover cold smelt can also be marinated.

1 lb (500 g) fillets of smelt
butter and oil
bread crumbs
salt
pepper

Stuffing:
I chopped parsley, lemon juice
II chopped dill, tomato purée
III chopped chives
IV finely chopped onion and tomato purée

Sift bread crumbs on a piece of paper towel and spread out half the fillets of smelt, meaty side up. Sprinkle with salt and put about ½—1 tbsp of anyone stuffing on each fish. Cover with remaining smelts, skin side up; sprinkle with salt and sift bread crumbs over them. Fry in a mixture of oil and butter until golden brown on both sides. The breaded fish can also be broiled. Broil about 3 minutes on each side.

Marinated smelt

4 servings

15 left-over stuffed fillets of smelt

Marinade:
1¾ cup (4½ dl) pickling vinegar
1¼ cup (3 dl) water
½ cup (1 dl) sugar
1 tsp crushed allspice
3 sliced onions
bay leaf
dill

Boil vinegar, water, sugar, allspice and bay leaf. Cool. Layer smelt, sliced onions and dill and pour marinade over. Marinate over night. Serve cold with crisp bread and butter.

Through its secretive life in the deep and foreign waters, the eel has originated many tales. In Scandinavia for example one often says about an unreliable person that he is slippery as an eel.

Fish au gratin
6 servings

2 lb (1 kg) fillets of sole, flounder or pike
salt
dash of pepper
3 tbsp lemon juice
1 tbsp butter
**4½ oz (135 g) can shrimp or mussels or the
    same amount coarsely chopped shrimp**

Sauce:
2 tbsp butter
1 tbsp flour
1½ cup (3½ dl) fish stock and light cream
2 egg yolks
2—3 tbsp cold butter
salt
dash of pepper
2 tbsp grated cheese

Preheat oven to 425°. Sprinkle fillets with salt
and pepper. Place in buttered baking dish,
pour lemon juice over, dot with butter.
Cover with aluminium foil and bake for
10 minutes. Remove from oven and cool.
Pour off fish stock. Garnish with shrimp
or mussels.

Melt butter in saucepan, stir in flour gradually, add fish stock and cream. Simmer
5 minutes. Remove from heat and stir in
egg yolks and cold butter. Heat but do not
boil, stirring constantly. Remove from heat
and stir until thick. Season. Pour over fish.

Force Mashed potatoes, see recipe beside,
through pastry bag along edge of fish platter.
Sprinkle with grated cheese. Place under
broiler or in very hot oven, 475°, and bake
for 10 minutes or until golden brown.

It took a long time before it was known where the
eel laid their roe, but now one knows that the eel
spawns develop in the Sea of Sargasso. Later they
follow the streams towards the coasts of Europe.

Mashed potatoes

3 medium-sized potatoes
water
salt
1 tbsp butter
¼ cup (½ dl) milk
2 egg yolks
salt
pepper
dash of nutmeg

Peel potatoes and boil in salted water until soft. Drain. Mash thoroughly or put through a blender. Add butter; gradually add milk and work until smooth. Add egg yolks and beat until light and fluffy. Season.

Fish au gratin

It takes up to ten years before the eel is full grown and fat. Thereafter they leave Scandinavia and return to the place where they came from. The eel migration is taken place at night and in very

Herring with onion sauce
4 servings

Salt herring was the mainstay of Scandinavia's diet during the winter months until the turn of the century. Rye flour makes the fish crusty and gives it a particular flavor. The onion sauce, which is surprisingly mild, goes very well with the salty fish.

6 fillets of salt herring
rye flour or unseasoned bread crumbs
butter and oil

Onion sauce:
3 large onions
2 oz (60 g) butter
3 tbsp flour
2 cups (5 dl) milk, or milk and cream mixed
salt, pepper
(soy sauce)

Wash fillets of herring and soak over night. Drain well on paper towel and bread with rye flour (or unseasoned bread crumbs). Fry in a mixture of oil and butter until golden brown on both sides. Keep hot and make onion sauce.

Slice onions and sauté slowly in butter. Blend in flour and add milk, stirring constantly over low heat until sauce has thickened. Season, but be careful with the salt; the herring will be quite salty. Serve with boiled potatoes.

Salt herring au gratin
4 servings

Salt herring au gratin becomes quite juicy with a rich custard. The potatoes retain some of their crunchiness and the herring gives it just the right amount of saltiness.

3 fillets of salt herring
2 finely chopped onions
2 tbsp butter
6 large potatoes
5 eggs
1¾ cup (4 dl) milk
½ tsp coarsely ground pepper

Soak herring fillets 8 hours or over night. Boil potatoes (do not peel them) and let them cool. Rinse and dry herring fillets and cut them into small pieces. Peel potatoes and slice them thinly. Cook onions in 1 tbsp butter until they are tender but not browned. Preheat oven to 375—400°. Butter a deep ovenware dish. Layer potatoes, chopped onions and herring, with potatoes as a bottom and top layer. Mix eggs and milk, season with pepper and pour this custard over the potatoes. Cook for 40 minutes. Serve with browned butter and a salad.

deep waters, often far from the coasts. Normally, the eel fishing season starts when the days are slowly getting darker, in the middle of September, and one usually talks about the "eel darkness".

Herring balls

4 servings

2 fillets of salt herring
4 medium-sized potatoes
⅔ cup (1½ dl) cooked, left-over meat
1 onion
1 tbsp cornstarch
3—4 tbsp milk
a few turns on your pepper mill (or a dash of ground pepper)
4 tbsp bread crumbs
butter

Soak fillets of herring for 8 hours or over night. Boil potatoes (do not peel them) and let them cool. Peel cold potatoes and put them through a blender together with dried herring fillets and left-over meat. The mixture should be coarsely ground, not puréed. Stir in cornstarch and milk. Season with pepper, no salt should be needed. Form mixture into balls, the size of a walnut. Roll them in bread crumbs and fry them in butter until they are hot and nicely browned. Serve with a salad and with Sweet and sour currant sauce, see recipe beside, and boiled potatoes.

Sweet sour currant sauce

4 servings

This sauce is served only with Herring balls, see recipe beside. The mixture is an odd one; at a glance it seems more Chinese or Middle Eastern than Scandinavian. But Scandinavian cooking contains many sweet and sour dishes. A fanciful guess would be that the Vikings acquired a taste for this kind of seasoning and brought it home from their Eastern travels. A more likely explanation is that the sweet and sour mixtures are a left-over from Medieval cookery; recipes from the Middle ages often require both sugar (honey) and vinegar and a lot of spices to boot.

⅓ cup (1 dl) currants (or ordinary raisins, if you can't find the small variety)
1⅔ cup (4 dl) stock
2 tbsp cornstarch
2—3 tbsp cold water
2 tbsp vinegar
1 tbsp syrup
(salt, soy sauce)
1 tbsp butter

Simmer currants in stock until they are soft, about 20 minutes. Dissolve cornstarch in a few tablespoons cold water. Pour cornstarch mixture into the boiling stock, stirring until the sauce has thickened. Season with vinegar, syrup, (salt and soy sauce) and stir in 1 tbsp butter.

"Sill" and "strömming" are really the same fish, herring. What it is called depends on where it is caught. In Finland and on the Swedish east coast it is called "strömming", otherwise always "sill".

Quenelles from Norway
4 servings

Well made quenelles are a treat—airy and light and succulent. They're also time-consuming to make; if you take the trouble to make them at all, you may as well use fresh fish. If you buy fish whole and have it cleaned, take home bones, heads and fins to use for the stock. If the fish is already cut into fillets, you can buy some inexpensive fish for your stock, or simply use salted water.

1½ lb (700 g) fillets of haddock, cod or
    whiting
2 tsp salt
½—1 tsp ground pepper
dash of nutmeg
1 egg white
1 tbsp cornstarch or potato flour
1 cup (2½ dl) milk
1 cup (2½ dl) whipping cream

Fish stock:
4 cups (1 l) water
heads, fins and bones of fish
1 quartered onion
1 sliced carrot
salt
whole pepper (1 clove)

Cut fish into small pieces and put through a blender. It should be pureed. Work the fish into a smooth paste and gradually and carefully add 1 egg white and the cornstarch.

Season with salt, pepper and a dash of nutmeg. Now gradually and carefully add 1 cup (2½ dl) milk and 1 cup (2½ dl) whipping cream. Keep ingredients cool and stir evenly and carefully. When all ingredients are blended the consistency of the mixture should be like a firm cream.

Meanwhile boil fish heads, spices and vegetables in 4 cups (1 l) water. Strain stock. Shape fish mixture into balls. Have ready 2 tablespoons. Dip one in hot water, with the other scoop up enough of the quenelle-mixture to form a spoon-sized ball. Lightly pat the ball and even it with the hot spoon. Drop quenelles into hot stock and simmer very gently — do not boil — until they are done and float up, 5—8 minutes.

Norwegians serve their quenelles with a béchamel sauce made of the strained fish stock and seasoned with horse-radish or curry. A good cream sauce (a béchamel sauce enriched with cream) seasoned with shrimp, lobster or oysters would taste even better.

The Swedes like to eat lingonberry preserves with fried fish. Whipped cream mixed with lingonberry preserves is served with fried herring and is considered to be a delicacy in many places. In other

Creamed perch
4 servings

This is a simple, classic recipe for perch. Supposedly it was invented at Blå Porten, The Blue Gate, a Stockholm restaurant famous in the 1890's.

4 medium-sized perch, about 2 lb (1 kg)
2 tbsp butter
2 tbsp flour
1 cup (2—3 dl) water and table cream mixed
2 tsp salt
dash of pepper
1 bay leaf
dash of thyme
parsley and/or dill

Have fish scaled and cleaned. Ordinarily it is used whole, with the head left on. If you don't want to bone the fish at the table you can use perch fillets instead.

Season fish with salt and pepper and put a generous amount of parsley and/or dill inside. Butter a pot and put the fish in, stomach down, backs up; pack them close together so they support each other. Gradually add cold water and cream to flour until it becomes a thin paste. Pour over fish. Add bay leaf (and thyme). If you are using fillets, add parsley and/or dill. Cover and simmer gently. Shake or tilt pot from time to time so the fish doesn't burn. Whole fish is done in 10—15 minutes, fillets in 5—7 minutes. Serve with baked or boiled potatoes.

Pike with horse-radish
4 servings

1 pike, 2—2½ lb (1—1¼ kg)
1 tbsp salt
4 cups (1 l) water
1 tbsp salt
1 onion
5 grains of pepper
parsley

Sauce:
2—3 oz (75 g) butter
grated horse-radish

Garnish:
parsley
1 lemon

Have fish cleaned and scaled. If the head is left on (that's how it's usually served in Scandinavia) the gills must be cut out. Rub fish with salt inside and out and leave for 10 minutes. Boil water, salt, pepper, parsley and sliced onion. Simmer pike gently for 20 minutes or until done. Strain and garnish with parsley and sliced lemon. Melt butter, blend in grated horse-radish to taste (and season with a little lemon juice). Serve with boiled potatoes.

parts of Scandinavia the combination is looked upon as barbaric. If you don't dare to try this combination, mix instead chopped dill and parsley with cream or sour cream, and serve with fried herring.

Fish in aspic
4 servings

Fish in aspic is a common dish in Scandinavia. Mainly it's mackerel which is prepared in this fashion, but eel and other kinds of fish not commonly available in the U.S may also be used. Shellfish or shrimp are sometimes added to the mold for looks and taste. It's an excellent party dish, prepared in advance, and it's both good looking and good to eat. Serve with a mayonnaise or tartar sauce, with hot rolls and a salad.

Stock:
for every 4 cups (1 l) water, take:
1 tbsp salt
2 tbsp vinegar
3 grains whole pepper
2 tbsp gelatin for every 3½ cup (8½ dl) of stock
5 grains allspice
1 bay leaf
2 tbsp coarsely chopped dill

Rinse fish and cut into 2—3″ (5—7 cm) pieces. Mix ingredients for stock. Boil stock for 10 minutes, correct seasoning; it should have a good, strong, somewhat sour taste. Simmer fish until tender but do not let it boil. Mackerel should be done in less than 10 minutes. Remove from stock. Strain stock. There should be about 3½ cup (8 dl). If there isn't enough, add water, lemon juice or a little bit of vinegar. Soak gelatin in ¼ cup (½ dl) cold stock. Dissolve in heated stock.

Chill until it begins to thicken.

Skin fish and remove bones, but leave it in large pieces. Put a layer of aspic in a wet mold, arrange pieces of fish on top, garnish with dill, with pieces of celery, with shrimp or thin slices of carrot. Pour a layer of aspic over fish. Repeat until mold is filled. The last layer should be aspic. Chill. Unmold and serve.

Horse-radish cream

To serve with duck, cold fish in aspic, cold salmon.

½ cup (1 dl) whipping cream
½ tbsp vinegar
1 tsp sugar
1 tbsp grated horse-radish (or the same amount prepared horse-radish from a jar)

Whip cream until it is thick but not stiff. Mix in other ingredients. Chill and serve. Horse-radish cream is sometimes served frozen, almost like serving a spicy ice-cream with your cold fish. If you want to try it, whip cream until it is almost stiff, add other ingredients and freeze in a tray. Spoon into a bowl and serve.

Herring is the most important fish in the Scandinavian waters. More than any other fish it has played a role in peoples' fantasy and in folklore. The ways of preparing herring are many and varying.

Bacalao casserole

6—8 servings

This delicious dried salt cod dish is called Bacalao, the name under which it is exported to Spanish-speaking countries.

1 lb (500 g) salt dried cod
6—8 medium-sized raw potatoes
4 medium-sized onions
¼ fresh Spanish pepper pod
⅔ cup (1½ dl) tomato purée
¾ cup (2 dl) oil
¾ cup (2 dl) water

Garnish:
2 tomatoes
2 tbsp chopped parsley

Rinse fish and soak 2 days, changing water a few times. Remove skin and bones, and cut fish into small squares. Peel potatoes and slice. Peel and slice onion and parboil a few minutes. Layer in deep saucepan or heavy kettle: potato slices, fish, onion, pepper and tomato purée. Pour in oil and cold water. Cover and simmer carefully 45 minutes or until potatoes and fish are tender. Do not stir, but shake pan occasionally. Serve hot, garnished with tomato slices and chopped parsley.

Fish soufflé

4 servings

1 lb (500 g) cleaned cod or haddock
2 cups (5 dl) water
1 tbsp lemon juice
1 tsp salt
5 grains of pepper

Cream sauce:
2 tbsp butter
3 tbsp flour
1¼ cup (3 dl) fish stock
dash of nutmeg
3 eggs
2 tbsp chopped parsley
(3 tbsp capers)

Preheat oven to 350°. Simmer fish slowly in water seasoned with lemon, salt and pepper. Strain, reserve stock and reduce it to about 1¼ cup (3 dl). Melt butter, stir in flour and add reduced fish stock, stirring constantly until sauce has thickened. Remove from heat and stir in 3 beaten egg yolks with nutmeg, parsley (capers and more salt) and fish in small flakes. Season well. Cool.

Beat egg whites until stiff and fold them lightly into the fish mixture. Pour into a well greased soufflé or other dish with straight, high edges. Bake until firm, 45—60 minutes. Serve the soufflé with brown butter or with chilled spiced butter.

There used to be plenty of salmon in the rivers and streams all over Scandinavia; salmon, together with herring and smelt, were the mainstay of the Scandinavian diet. Farmhands used to demand a

Norwegian fish mousse
6 servings

1½ lb (700 g) fillets of haddock, cod or pike
2 tbsp salt
1 tsp pepper
dash of nutmeg
1½ tbsp cornstarch
1⅓ cup (3½ dl) milk
1½ cup (3½ dl) table cream

Dry fish fillets and put them through
a blender. Work purée until it is smooth.
Stir in cornstarch and seasoning, then
gradually add milk and cream. The mixture
should be like an even, heavy cream. Check
the seasoning. Preheat oven to 375°.

Pour mixture into a buttered and breaded
pudding mold, 8″ (20 cm) in diameter.
Cover mold with aluminium foil. Put a deep
baking dish into the oven and fill it to about
¾ with boiling water. Place the pudding
mold in the hot water and cook 45—60
minutes or until the mousse is set. Check
the water a few times and add more if
needed. Unmold carefully on a hot platter
and garnish with parsley, sautéed mushrooms or shrimp. Serve with browned butter
or a good shrimp sauce.

Marinated salmon

clause in their contract explicity stating that
they wouldn't have to eat salmon more than four
times a week. These days no one is condemned to
a diet of salmon, on the contrary, it's an expen-

Marinated salmon

6—8 servings

2 lb or more (1 kg) fresh salmon (not frozen); pick a piece from the middle of the fish where it's thick

For every lb (½ kg) fish:
2—3 tbsp salt
2—3 tbsp sugar
10 grains coarsely crushed pepper
⅔ cup (1½ dl) cut fresh dill

Scrape fish clean with a knife and dry on paper towel. Do not wash. Cut the fish open along its back ridge: remove backbone. Rub fish (both the meat and the skin side) with salt and sugar. Sprinkle with coarsely ground pepper. Cover the bottom of a shallow pan with dill and put one piece of fish on top, skin side down. Cover meat side with dill, place other piece of fish on top, skin side up. The thick part of the upper fillet will now be resting on the thin part of the bottom fillet, exactly opposite to the way the pieces were originally joined. Cover with remaining dill. Marinate in refrigerator at least 48 hours.

Marinated salmon will keep in the refrigerator for a week. To serve: scrape off pepper and dill and cut salmon into thin slices, without cutting all the way through the skin. This way the fish is skinned before serving. (Thin strips of skin from marinated salmon are sometimes broiled and served as a garnish along with the fish.)

Traditionally marinated salmon is served with toast and butter, lemon wedges, or a special sauce (see recipe below). Sometimes marinated salmon is served as an hors d'oeuvre. If the salmon is to be eaten as an entrée, allow 4—5 oz (120—150 g) per person; allow 2—3 oz (60—90 g) if it is served as hors d'oeuvre.

Sauce for marinated salmon

Sufficient for 2 lb (1 kg) fish

1 tbsp vinegar
2 tbsp sugar
6 tbsp mustard (pick a sour variety, or use Dijon mustard)
⅔ cup (1½ dl) oil
2 tbsp finely chopped fresh dill

Mix vinegar, sugar and mustard. Gradually add oil one drop at a time while stirring constantly, just as if you were making a mayonnaise. Stir in dill.

How to marinate other fish
Any fat fish can be marinated in the same fashion as salmon. Mackerel is often served marinated in Scandinavia. The fish must be fresh, though, not frozen or thawed.

sive fish and a gourmet treat, served only at special occasions. Such an occasion is Midsummer, the summer solstice on June 21, when marinated or boiled salmon is a traditional part of the celebrations.

Shellfish salad

4 servings

A shellfish salad is often served on a smör-gåsbord, or as a party dish for a light supper. Scandinavian shrimp can only be bought canned in the U.S., and are not as good as the fresh ones. They are hard to find outside of specialty stores. Use American shrimp or crab meat instead.

Gently mix:
1½ cup (3½ dl) chopped shrimp or crabmeat
(1 can (4½ oz) (135 g) well drained mussels)
1½ cup (3½ dl) sliced raw mushrooms
1 cup (2½ dl) tiny sweet peas (if canned, drain well)
½ cup (1 dl) cubed cucumber
2 hard-boiled eggs

Dressing:
¼ cup (½ dl) vinegar
½ cup (1 dl) oil
salt
coarsely ground pepper
2 tbsp finely chopped dill

Pour the dressing over the salad mixture and refrigerate for a few hours. Serve salad on a bed of crisp, coarsely cut lettuce and garnish with slices of hard-boiled eggs.

Old-fashioned dressing

Scandinavia has interesting salad dressings. They are sometimes served with cold, boiled or marinated fish, but will taste good with any of your favorite salads.

1 hard-boiled egg yolk
1 raw egg yolk
2 tbsp mustard
1 tsp vinegar
salt
pepper
1 cup (2½ dl) whipped cream

Mash hard-boiled egg yolk and cream together with raw egg yolk, mustard and spices. Carefully fold in whipped cream. Serve cold.

In late summer the shellfish season starts with the catching of fresh water crayfish, salt water crayfish, crabs, lobsters and mussels. The fresh water crayfish is considered a special delicacy.

Crayfish

Scandinavians rave about crayfish. Crayfish are quite expensive and may only be caught during a few weeks in July and August. The crayfish feast is a set ritual. Scandinavian aquavit and beer are served along with the crayfish, and toast and butter, but nothing else—no sauces, no dressing, nothing. A real crayfish party is held out of doors. It's an evening in August, the nights are quite dark by then: there should be a moon, a bit of fog from the nearby lake, and paper lanterns. It's getting chilly, the summer is over, but there will be raspberries picked in the woods nearby for dessert, or sweet wild blueberries.

Crayfish is common in some parts of the United States: in many areas you can fish them yourself in almost any creek. You can also order them shipped air-mail from large fishing companies in Wisconsin or New Orleans. Even if you have them flown in, crayfish are less expensive in the U.S. than in Scandinavia.

Crayfish, in case you've never seen one, look like small lobsters. You eat the tail, suck on the head, and crack open the tiny claws. It tastes somewhat like lobster, but the meat is finer, and never stringy. If it seems like too much trouble to catch crayfish or order them, you can taste something similar by using Maryland Blue crab instead. The crab won't taste exactly the same, but it will be close if prepared the way Scandinavians cook their crayfish. Use medium to large crabs and allow half a dozen per serving.

How to cook crayfish
Allow a dozen or more per serving. Wash crayfish well in running water. They have to be alive, just like crabs. Use heavy duty gloves or tongs when handling them. Have ready a large pot of boiling water. For every quart (1 l) of water add 2 tbsp salt and 1 tbsp dill seeds, Scandinavians always use fresh dill that's gone to seed.

Drop 8—10 crayfish at a time into the boiling water. Cover. When the water starts boiling again, drop in another 8—10 crayfish. About 4 dozen can be boiled in one pot. Cook 5 more minutes from the last time the water starts to boil. Remove from heat and chill the crayfish in the water they've been boiling in. If you need the pot for another batch, pour out the crayfish and water into a large jar and start over. Don't keep using the same water, since it will get too salty. Chill completely. Arrange into a mound on a large platter and garnish with fresh dill that's gone to seed. Treat crabs the same way. Chill and serve.

The salt water crayfish is considerably cheaper than the fresh water and has been highly appreciated in the last few years. You buy it alive and cook it yourself if you live in the parts where it's caught.

Wintertime in Northern Scandinavia

Soups

Beef broth

4 servings

about 2 lb (1 kg) beef shank
6 cups (1½ l) cold water
2 tsp salt
5 grains of pepper
2 cloves
5 medium-sized potatoes
1 large carrot
1 turnip
2 leeks or onions or a bunch or spring onions
parsley

Cover meat with cold water and bring slowly
to a boil. Skim well. Season, cover and
simmer gently for 45 minutes. Now add
sliced potatoes, carrot, leeks or onions.
Continue simmering until meat and vegetables are done. (Meanwhile prepare dumplings.) Remove meat, discard any fat, cut
into bit-sized pieces, and put back into the
broth. Check seasoning. Serve with dumplings and chopped parsley.

Dumplings

4 servings

1½ tbsp butter
4 tbsp flour
1¾ cup (4 dl) milk
2 egg yolks
2 tbsp grated cheese
a dash of grated cardamon or a drop of
  almond flavoring

Melt butter over low heat and blend in flour.
Add milk, stirring constantly until sauce has
thickened. Remove from heat. Beat together
egg yolks and 1—2 tbsp milk, add a little of
the sauce to this mixture and blend well.
Return this mixture to the rest of the sauce
and cook over low heat, stirring vigorously
until sauce is hot, thick and well blended.
Stir in cheese and cardamon or almond
flavoring. Let cool.

Bring 4—6 cups (1—1½ l) of salted water to
a rapid boil. Reduce heat. Gently drop
dumplings the size of a quarter into the hot
water and simmer for 4—5 minutes. Remove,
drain and serve in the broth. The seasoning—
cardamon or almond—together with beef
broth is unusual and interesting. Exactly
the same dumplings, minus cheese, are used
in sweet dessert soups—another Scandinavian speciality, see page 65.

Soup belongs to the good old home cooking. Beef
broth with dumplings is a dish which should be
served steaming hot on cold days. Such a soup is
not only hot and refreshing, it's also economical.

Salmon soup

4 servings

½ lb (250 g) fresh (preferably not frozen)
  salmon
½ lb (250 g) potatoes
4 cups (1 l) water
½ cup (1 dl) chopped onion
1 cup (2½ dl) whipping cream
3 tbsp chopped dill
salt
pepper
allspice
2 tbsp butter

The original recipe calls for fish stock. If you
buy fresh salmon you can have it cleaned,
but take home bones, fins and skin and boil
them in 4 cups (1 l) of water. Season with
a piece of celery, salt, pepper, one sliced
onion and some dill. The soup tastes good
even if you don't start with preparing a fish
stock, but use 4 cups (1 l) of plain water.

Peel and slice potatoes. Boil them together
with chopped onions, salt, pepper and a few
grains of coarsely crushed allspice, until
they are very tender. Clean and wash salmon
and cut it in bit-sized pieces. Put them in
the soup and simmer gently until they are
done. Add cream and dill, correct seasoning
and heat. Add 2 tbsp butter just before
serving.

Mushroom soup

4 servings

½ lb (250 g) fresh mushrooms
2 tbsp butter
salt
pepper
2 tbsp flour
5 cups (1¼ l) stock and mushroom juice
⅓ cup (1 dl) whipping cream
½ tsp lemon juice
(1—2 tbsp Madeira or sherry)
(1 tsp grated onion)

Rinse mushrooms and cut into slices. Cook
mushrooms in their own juices until soft.
Strain off cooking liquid. Add butter and
sauté mushrooms over low heat. Season.
Sprinkle flour over them and add liquid.
Simmer for 5 minutes. Add cream and lemon
juice. Wine and grated onion can also be
added. Taste for seasoning.

Dumplings can be prepared in many different ways.
The recipes are often local and the seasoning
varies. In the north of Scandinavia they prefer
to serve dumplings with the taste of almonds.

Brown cabbage soup

4 servings

1 large head of cabbage
2 oz (75 g) butter
1 tbsp brown sugar
4 cups (1 l) stock
1 tsp salt
½ tsp crushed pepper
½ tsp crushed allspice
parsley

Shred cabbage. Melt butter in heavy pan and sauté cabbage over low heat. Stir constantly until cabbage is nicely browned. Add sugar and spices, cover and simmer gently for about 30 minutes. Add stock and continue simmering until cabbage is very tender. Sprinkle with chopped parsley before serving.

This soup is often served with small meatballs, called "frikadeller". Prepare half a batch of Meatballs, see page 6. Boil 6 cups (1½ l) of salted water. Turn down heat and boil meatballs gently for 6—8 minutes. Remove, drain and put them in the soup. They can also be boiled directly in the cabbage soup, but will cloud the stock.

Kale soup

4 servings

This hearty green soup used to be frequent winter food and is still quite popular all over Scandinavia.

2 lb (1 kg) kale
2 cups (5 dl) water
1 tsp salt
4 tbsp chopped chives or onion
1 tbsp butter
1½ tbsp flour
4 cups (1 l) pork stock plus cooking liquid from kale
salt
pepper

Wash kale leaves well and drain. Cook in salted water for 10 minutes or until soft. Strain, reserving liquid. Chop kale and chives finely or put through a mixer. Melt butter, add flour and stir until well blended. Add stock, stirring, and simmer 5 minutes. Add kale and chives and reheat. Season. Serve with poached eggs or hard-boiled eggs cut in halves.

When it's rainy and cold outside, and the wind is blowing hard, the steaming hot soup tastes lovely. You can make a soup from left-overs or anything handy. A rich brown cabbage soup or a fish soup.

Yellow pea soup

Dried yellow peas, a Scandinavian speciality, taste much like split peas. You may find them in Scandinavian grocery stores. They are by far the more common variety in Scandinavia. Yellow pea soup is

Split pea soup
4 servings

1⅔ cup (4 dl) split peas
2 quarts (2 l) water
½ lb (250 g) lean cured ham or pork
1 onion
(2 carrots)
thyme
salt

Wash peas and soak in 2 quarts (2 l) of
water over night. Bring to a rapid boil and
skim. Chop onion, (slice carrots) and add to
peas together with seasoning and meat.
Cover and simmer gently until peas and meat
are done, 1—1½ hours. Remove meat, cut it
into small pieces and put them back into
the soup. Check seasoning before serving.

Yellow pea soup
4 servings

1⅔ cup (4 dl) dried yellow peas
2 quarts (2 l) water
½ lb (250 g) lean cured ham or pork
1 onion
(2 carrots)
marjoram
salt

Prepare Yellow pea soup as you would Split
pea soup, but season with marjoram instead
of thyme. Hot mustard is usually served with
the ham. Both soups can be prepared in
large quantities and frozen.

traditionally served every Thursday, followed by
pancakes or "plättar", tiny pancakes cooked on a
special griddle. On festive occasions the soup
is often served with a hot, sweet Swedish Punch.

Nettle soup
4 servings

In Scandinavia, fresh nettles are sold in grocery stores. If you want to taste nettle soup in the U.S., you'll have to pick the nettles yourself. They should be picked when they first come up, in very early spring, when the leaves are tiny, light green, and tender and the stems still soft. They may be hard to find, but if you know of a spot where they grow, you may check for the first shoots in February or March, depending on where you live. Nettle soup has a delicate, spinach-like flavor and is said to be very good for you—at least as good as spinach. For Scandinavians it's a great delicacy, something to look forward to each year: once the nettles are out, spring cannot be far away. Please pick with gloves—even tiny nettles sting badly. Once they are boiled, though, they are perfectly safe to eat.

6 cups (1½ l) tiny nettles
6 cups (1½ l) chicken stock
3 tbsp flour
1½ tbsp butter
salt
pepper
½ tsp crushed aniseeds or fennel
1 tbsp chopped chives

Clean nettles; remove wilted leaves and coarse stems. Rinse very well. Blanch in 1 cup (2½ dl) salted water. Strain, reserving liquid, and put through a mixer. It should be a coarse purée—don't grind them too finely. Melt butter over low heat and blend in flour. Add stock, stirring constantly. Add liquid from nettles together with ground nettles and season. Serve with a poached egg in each plate, or with hard-boiled quartered or sliced eggs.

Green peas are common in Finland. The soup can be made in the same way as yellow pea soup. In the "old days" a very thick, green pea soup was served to farm hands and soldiers together with salted herring.

Summer vegetable soup

4 servings

For Scandinavians this soup is a great summer treat—once upon a time it was made with the first tender vegetables from their gardens, which they'd been waiting for all spring. Today vegetables of any kind are available all through the year. But the soup remains a favorite; it has a mild, slightly sweet taste.

1 bunch of tiny fresh carrots
1 stalk of celery
1 bunch of spring onions
1 cup (2 dl) fresh green peas
1 small head of cauliflower
salt
4 cups (1 l) milk
2—3 tbsp butter
½ cup (1 dl) table cream
½ cup (1 dl) chopped parsley

Clean vegetables, slice carrots, celery, and onions and break cauliflower into small pieces. Blanch vegetables in 1 cup (2½ dl) salted water. Reserve liquid. Melt 2 tbsp butter, blend in flour and add milk, stirring constantly over low heat. Add vegetables and the water they were blanched in. Season with salt; stir in cream and remaining butter and garnish with chopped parsley. Vegetables should be crisp and barely done. An extra dot of butter in each plate will enhance the flavor of the vegetables.

Finnish cucumber soup

⅓—½ cup (1 dl) butter
1 small chopped onion
4 medium-sized cucumbers
3 tbsp flour
6 cups (1½ l) chicken stock
dash of pepper
2 egg yolks
1 tbsp dry sherry
1 cup (2½ dl) table cream
3 tbsp chopped parsley

Melt butter in saucepan and add onion and peeled and sliced cucumbers. Simmer for 10 minutes, stirring frequently. Sprinkle with flour and mix well. Gradually add chicken stock and pepper and simmer another 10 minutes, stirring constantly. Beat soup until smooth. Beat egg yolks, sherry and cream. Gradually stir into soup. Season and add parsley. Cucumber soup is served chilled.

In the spring the holidays come close. The eve of May Day, the Ascension Day and the Whitsun holiday are such holidays when the nettle soup or the summer vegetable soup are perfect dishes to start with.

Cloudberry mire in the north

Desserts

Fruit soup

4 servings

½ lb (200 g) mixed, pared fruit
5 cups (1¼ l) water
(lemon)
1 piece cinnamon
⅓ cup (1 dl) sugar or more, depending on
    tartness of fruit
2 tbsp cornstarch

Simmer fruit with sugar and cinnamon until
tender. For apples, pears, strawberries and
other sweet fruit, add juice from ½ lemon
and a piece of lemon rind. Thin cornstarch
with ¼ cup (½ dl) cold water, let soup come
to a rapid boil and stir in cornstarch mixture.
The soup can be served hot or cold. Rose
hip soup (which you may find packaged in
Scandinavian grocery stores) is usually
served lukewarm together with whipped
cream and slivered almonds.

Rhubarb pie

4 servings

Pie crust with egg:
1 cup (1½ dl) flour
3 tbsp sugar
1 egg yolk
4 oz (125 g) butter
(1 egg)

Rhubarb filling:
1 lb (500 g) rhubarb
½ cup (1¼ dl) sugar or more depending
    on taste
1 tbsp cornstarch

Mix flour and sugar and cut in butter. Add
egg yolk and gather into a ball. Cool for about
1 hour. Preheat oven to 425°. Roll out ⅔ of
the dough and line bottom and sides of a
pie dish. Bake for 10 minutes. Remove from
oven. Clean and cut rhubarb in 1" (2.5 cm)
long pieces. Mix with cornstarch and sugar
and fill into pie shell. Roll remaining dough
into strips and weave a lattice work on top of
the filling. Brush with egg and bake for
another 20 minutes or until done. Serve
lukewarm with whipped cream, vanilla ice
cream or vanilla custard, see page 66.

The classic dessert soup was made from mixed dried
fruit which was soaked and then boiled in the same
water. It was popular at a time when fresh fruit
was an expensive luxury during the winter months.

Swedish apple cake
4 servings

This is a very old-fashioned dessert. Traditionally confectioner's sugar used to be sprinkled in a pattern on top of the cake. To make the pattern, cut a piece of stiff paper in the shape of the bottom of the pan. Now fold this rounded sheet of paper three times, so that it's folded in eighths. Cut holes, squares and crescent shapes into the layers of paper. Unfold. You should have an even, lacy-looking pattern. Place on cool cake and sift confectioner's sugar over it. Remove pattern carefully. Cutting paper patterns was something children were asked to do.

2 cups (5 dl) unseasoned bread crumbs or cracker crumbs
3 oz (75—100 g) butter
1⅔—2 cups (4—5 dl) tart apple sauce
confectioner's sugar

Preheat oven to 400°. Butter a ring mold (with removable rim). Reserve about ½ tbsp butter. Sauté bread crumbs lightly in remaining butter. Put a layer of bread crumbs on the bottom of the pan, spread apple sauce on top, add another layer of bread crumbs, spread another layer of apple sauce, and top with bread crumbs. Bake for 30 minutes. Serve warm or cold, sprinkled with confectioner's sugar. Custard sauce is usually served with it, see recipe beside.

Custard sauce
4 servings

¾ cup (2 dl) table cream
1—2 tsp vanilla
3 egg yolks
2 tbsp sugar
¾ cup (2 dl) whipping cream

Heat table cream. Beat egg yolks and sugar until mixture is foamy. Beating continuously, pour hot cream over mixture. Pour into double boiler (or simmer over low heat) and continue beating until mixture has thickened. Let cool and stir from time to time. Stir in vanilla. Whip cream and fold gently into the sauce. Serve chilled.

Today grocery stores in Scandinavia sell as many varieties of fresh fruit all year round as do stores in the U.S. People prefer to eat the fruit fresh nowadays. Fruit soups are on their way out.

Danish fruit pudding

4 servings

1 lb (500 g) strawberries
2 tbsp sugar
⅓ cup (¾ dl) water
1½ tbsp cornstarch

Clean berries and rinse in a colander. Drain well. Mash with sugar and bring to a quick boil. Thin cornstarch with water and pour into hot strawberries, stirring constantly. Bring to another quick boil and remove from heat. Pour into a bowl and chill. (Sprinkle about 1 tbsp sugar on top to keep surface soft.) Serve cold with table cream.

Prune soufflé

4 servings

6—7 oz (200 g) pitted prunes
⅓ cup (1 dl) brown sugar
3—4 tbsp chopped almonds
1 tbsp cornstarch
4—5 egg whites

Preheat oven to 325°. Chop prunes and mix with almonds and sugar. Beat egg whites stiff. Sprinkle cornstarch on top, then gently fold in prune mixture. Pour into well buttered soufflé or other ovenware dish with high, straight sides. Cook for 30 minutes. Serve hot with chilled table cream or vanilla ice cream.

Wizard's pudding

6 servings

3 egg whites
1 cup (2½ dl) lingonberry or cranberry preserve
½ tbsp vanilla
2½ tbsp sugar

Beat egg whites until stiff. Add preserve, vanilla and sugar and beat vigorously until very light and fluffy, using electric mixer. Serve with milk or Vanilla custard, see page 66.

Fluffy berry pudding

4 servings

2 cups (5 dl) water
1 cup (2½ dl) sweetened raspberry or cranberry juice
½ cup (1 dl) cream of wheat

Boil water and juice. Gradually sprinkle cream of wheat into liquid beating vigorously to prevent lumps. Simmer for 5 minutes, stirring occasionally. Remove from heat and pour into mixer or large bowl. Beat well until cold and very fluffy. Pour into serving dish. Cool in refrigerator for ½ hour. Serve with milk or cream.

In the most gardens in Scandinavia you will find fruit trees and berry bushes like black and red currants, gooseberries and raspberries. Apples, pears as well as plums are growing way up north.

Rice pudding
8 servings

3 tsp gelatin
¼ cup (½ dl) water
⅓ cup (¾ dl) milk
⅓ cup (¾ dl) rice
2 tsp vanilla
2 oz (1 dl) almonds
5 tbsp sugar
4 tbsp butter
1¼ cup (3 dl) whipping cream

Wash rice and simmer gently (in a double boiler) in milk until it is very tender. Soak gelatin in ¼ cup (½ dl) cold water for 5 minutes. Dissolve over heat and stir into rice. Add vanilla, sugar, chopped almonds and creamed butter. Cool. Whip cream and fold into cold rice mixture. Put in a wet mold and chill until set, 6 hours or more. Unmold and serve with tart fruit juice, stewed fruit or hot butterscotch sauce (which is not Scandinavian, but tastes good with the rice pudding).

Royal meringues
4 servings

Meringues:
4 egg whites
½ cup (1¼ dl) sugar

Garnish:
2 ripe bananas
chocolate syrup
1¼ cup (3 dl) whipping cream

Preheat oven to 225°. Make meringues: beat egg whites (with an electric beater) until foamy. Add 1 tbsp sugar at a time and continue beating until the mixture stands in stiff spikes and the bowl can be turned upside-down. Drop mixture on ungreased cookie sheets and bake for 45 minutes or until dry. Let cool on cookie sheets for about 5 minutes before removing them.

Arrange cool meringues on a platter together with sliced bananas. Cover with whipped cream and garnish with chocolate syrup. Serve at once.

Most people who have access to a little piece of land plant a couple of rhubarb plants. The first rosy rhubarb stalks are used to make a delicious pie. A pie in Scandinavia doesn't taste the same

Royal meringues

as an English or American pie. The pie crust is
very crisp and cookie like. When the berries of
the wild woods ripen people like to go out and
pick them. Not only people living in the country

Cranberry pears

This is an old-fashioned dessert, the kind elderly people remember as a treat from their childhood. It's not often served today, though it is neither complicated nor expensive to make; but nowadays fresh fruit is available all year round, and Scandinavians often prefer an uncooked pear to a boiled compote. If you want to try — here is the recipe.

2 lb (1 kg) small pears (preferably seckels)
4 cups (1 l) water
2 cups (5 dl) sugar
1 cup (2½ dl) cranberry sauce (out of a can)
1 piece lemon peel
juice of 1 lemon

Peel pears and scrape stalk. The stalk is traditionally left on the pears which are left whole. Slowly boil sugar, water, cranberry sauce and lemon. Simmer pears in the syrup until they are barely done. Fill pears into crocks and strain the hot liquid over them. Cool and store in a cold place. Cranberry pears will keep for weeks. The rose-colored pears were traditionally served with whipped cream, or table cream and wafer-thin cookies. They are good and interesting as a topping for vanilla ice cream.

Ginger pears (preserve)

Pears should be barely ripe. Use seckels, the small, sweet, early variety
For every 2 lb (1 kg) of pears you'll need:
2 cups (5 dl) water
2 cups (5 dl) sugar
3 pieces of dried ginger

Boil sugar, water and ginger to a light syrup, 5—10 minutes. Peel pears and cut them in halves lengthwise. Remove seeds. Use a teaspoon and not a knife, otherwise it's difficult not to cut into the pear. Simmer pears very gently over low heat until they are transparent. They should keep their shape, which means that the heat has to be very low. It will take about 1 hour or slightly longer.

Remove pears and put them into crocks. Boil syrup until it has thickened slightly, another 10 minutes, and pour it hot over the pears. Cool and cover. Keep preserve in a cool and dry place. It will keep for almost 1 year. Traditionally it was served as a (Sunday) dessert together with whipped cream or table cream. It tastes very good together with ice cream.

or in the wooded areas, but also the city people. Blueberries and cloudberries are especially appreciated. But considered as the "biggest berry picking" are mainly the lingonberries and further

Scandinavian cheese cake
4 servings

6—7 oz (200 g) cottage cheese (small curd)
2 eggs
¾ cup (2 dl) table cream
1 tbsp sugar
½ tsp vanilla
3 tbsp chopped almonds

Preheat oven to 425°. Beat eggs lightly with cream. Put cheese through a sieve or through a blender, and mix in other ingredients. Pour into buttered ovenware dish and cook for 15—20 minutes. Serve hot with fruit preserve (and whipped cream).

Caramel custard
4 servings

Caramel:
1 cup (2½ dl) sugar
3 tbsp boiling water

Custard:
1¾ cup (4 dl) table cream
1 cup (2½ dl) milk
2 tbsp sugar
1 tsp vanilla or grated rind of ½ lemon
4 eggs
15 blanched almonds

Melt sugar in skillet over low heat until light brown syrup forms. Stir occasionally with wooden spoon until all lumps are gone. Slowly add boiling water and simmer until smooth. Coat bottom and sides of heated ring mold with caramel. Preheat oven to 300°.

Boil cream, milk and sugar in skillet used for preparing caramel. Remove from heat and add vanilla or lemon rind. Beat eggs in bowl and pour the hot milk mixture over, beating vigorously. Pour mixture into caramel-coated mold. Place deep oblong baking pan in oven and fill with hot water. Place mold in the water and bake for 45 minutes, or until custard is set. Chill, unmold and garnish with almonds.

up north the cloudberries. By tradition the Swedes, Finns and Norwegians have got their most important addition of vitamins from lingonberries and cloud-berries. The tradition of picking is still alive.

Apple cake

3 eggs
1½ cup (3½ dl) sugar
3 oz (100 g) butter
⅔ cup (1½ dl) milk
1¾ cup (4½ dl) flour
2½ tsp baking powder
4 tart apples
4 tbsp brown sugar
2 tsp cinnamon

Preheat oven to 400°. Grease and flour a
round baking pan, or bread it with unseasoned bread crumbs the way it's usually done
in Scandinavia. It gives the cake a slightly
crusty surface. Peel apples and slice thinly.
(Drip a little lemon juice over them if you're
not using them immediately, so that they
don't turn brown.) Beat eggs and sugar
until foamy. Melt butter, add milk and heat.
Pour the hot mixture over the eggs. Mix flour
with baking powder and add to egg mixture.
Pour into pan. Arrange apple slices on top
and sprinkle with brown sugar and cinnamon. Bake for 30 minutes or until done.

Waffles with cloudberry jam and cream

For today's people berry picking hasn't any eco-
nomical effect on the household, but is relaxing.
The berries are used for preserves and syrup and
become the foundation of many desserts wintertime.

Waffles
8 waffles

In Sweden the right time to eat waffles is in the spring. They are often served on March 25, the feast of the Annunciation, called "Marie Bebådelse", a Catholic holiday. Sweden has been Protestant since the fifteenhundreds, yet in some way or another has preserved many Catholic holidays— even if only for eating waffles.

Traditionally the waffles are served with whipped cream and cloudberry preserve. Cloudberries grow in Canada and in some of the northern states, and you may be able to find a jar in a Scandinavian grocery store. They have a very appetizing, golden color, and a peculiar, slightly malty taste, unlike any other berry. If you can't find them, any jam or fruit preserve will taste good with the waffles.

¾ cup (2 dl) water
1¼ cup (3 dl) flour
1¼ cup (3 dl) whipping cream
2 tbsp butter

Stir flour and water to make an even batter. Stir in melted butter. Whip cream and fold into flour mixture. (Use a wide-mouthed pitcher for mixing the batter so that it's easy to pour on the waffle iron. If you mix the batter in a bowl, use a large wooden spoon or ladle for pouring it on the iron.)

Heat a waffle iron. If you have an electric one, the indicator will tell you when it is ready to use. If you have a traditional Scandinavian iron that is put on the stove, only experience will tell you when you can start cooking the waffles. If the iron is properly broken in it shouldn't need any grease. Pour the grid surface about ⅔ full of batter. Close the lid and wait about 4 minutes. If you try to open the iron and it resists, that means the waffle is not quite done. Cook about 1 minute more and try again. The old-fashioned Scandinavian iron has to be turned on the stove. Cook waffles 2—3 minutes on each side.

Also in Scandinavia it is less common than in earlier times to serve desserts. The grown-ups have a cup of coffee after dinner and the children get an apple or an orange most of the time.

Pancakes
4 servings

Pancakes are best directly from the pan. In Scandinavia they are served with fresh berries mashed with sugar, or with jam or jelly or with lingonberry preserve. If you omit sugar in this recipe, the pancakes can be used with meat or vegetable fillings. They are delicious filled with creamed spinach and ham, then broiled with grated cheese on top. These pancakes come close to the famous French crêpes — the large thin pancakes which — depending on the filling — are served both as a main dish and as a dessert.

2 eggs
1 cup (2½ dl) flour
2½ cup (6 dl) milk
a pinch of salt
2 tsp sugar

Beat eggs with a little of the milk. Stir in flour and beat to an even mixture. Add remaining milk and stir in salt and sugar. If your griddle is well broken in it will need to be buttered only once or twice while you're cooking these pancakes.

Melt about 1 tsp of butter in griddle; pour batter, using a ladle, and tilt griddle so that it is evenly coated with a thin layer of batter. When bubbles appear on the surface, lift carefully with a spatula to see if cakes are browned. Turn only once. Fold or roll pancakes and keep them hot. Stir batter while cooking cakes so that the flour doesn't sink to the bottom of the bowl.

Plättar
are tiny pancakes, made from the same batter as the larger ones. You need a special griddle, called "plättlagg" in Swedish, which you may find in Scandinavian grocery stores. The "plättar" are usually served stacked — a stack of 8 is a normal serving.

But a dessert rounds off the dinner in a nice way. After a light main course as for example fish or soup one prefers to have a somewhat heavier dessert like a pie, apple cake, pancake or pudding.

Pancake torte

6—8 servings

This is an unusual way of making a torte. It is often served in the summer, layered with fresh blueberries, fresh sugared strawberries or red currants, and topped with whipped cream.

Prepare pancakes, see page 74. For a large, impressive torte you'll need a double batch. Cool pancakes. Spread fresh, sugared berries, apple sauce or jam between them and top with whipped cream. Cut into wedges, as you would any other torte. Not entirely Scandinavian, but delicous, is an American lemon or orange filling between the layers of pancakes. Use any recipe for pie filling, let cool and thicken so that it can be spread, and top with rum-flavored whipped cream.

Pancake from Finland

6 servings

4 eggs
½ cup (1 dl) sugar
1⅔—2 cups (4—5 dl) whipping cream
¾ cup (1¾ dl) flour
2 tbsp butter

Preheat oven to 425°. Beat eggs and sugar until foamy. Fold in flour. Whip cream and fold into egg mixture. Add melted butter. Pour batter into buttered skillet or ovenware pan and bake for about 20 minutes or until set. Serve warm with raspberry jam or other fruit preserve.

The most simple dessert is often the best liked. Most people like lingonberry preserves with milk for example. At more festive occasions it can be mixed with whipped cream and some bread crumbs.

Waving wheat field in the autumn

Baking

Miss Pihlgren's pretzels
40 pretzels

This is a very old recipe which comes from a handwritten collection handed down since the middle eighteen hundreds. The original recipe tells how you can make your own almond paste, a time-consuming process. Danish almond paste can be bought in most large grocery stores.

1 stick (125 g) butter
1 lb (250 g) almond paste
¾—1 cup (2—2½ dl) flour

Brush with:
1 egg

Sprinkle with:
chopped almonds and sugar

Preheat oven to 300°. Grate almond paste or put it through a blender and work in butter and flour. It should be a soft but manageable dough. Depending on how soft your almond paste is, you'll need a larger or smaller amount of flour. If the dough is too soft it's hard to handle. Roll out dough into a roll as thick as your middle finger, cut pieces 7—8″ (18—20 cm) long and form then into pretzels. Put pretzels on well greased cookie sheets, brush with lightly beaten egg and sprinkle with coarsely chopped almonds and sugar. Cook about 15 minutes.

Oatmeal cookies
40 cookies

1⅔ cup (4 dl) oatmeal
1 cup (2½ dl) flour
⅓ cup (1 dl) sugar
1⅔ stick (200 g) butter

Mix flour and oatmeal with sugar and cut in butter. Gather to a dough and chill for 1 hour. Preheat oven to 360°. Roll cookies about the size of a quarter, put them an inch apart on greased cookie sheet (they need room to expand while cooking). Press down on them lightly with a fork and cook for about 8 minutes.

The Scandinavian kitchen has a wealth of recipes for cookies. People cherish their recipes and they are still handed down from one generation to the next one, and in spite of the fact that excellent

Danish almond cookies
25 cookies

These traditional Danish cookies are very rich. They're excellent with ice cream or with a cup of coffee after dinner. They keep very well.

1 lb (450 g) almond paste
½ tsp almond flavoring
1—2 egg whites

Icing:
⅓ cup (1 dl) confectioner's sugar
½ tsp lemon juice
egg white

Preheat oven to 350°. Grate almond paste and mix in almond flavoring and egg whites. The mixture should be like a semi-soft dough. Roll into 1" (2.5 cm) thick rolls, about 2" (5 cm) long. Pinch one side to give them their characteristic triangular form. Cook for 6—8 minutes. The cookies should have a little bit of color but should be soft inside. Mix sugar, lemon juice and egg white for the icing (or use commercial icing in tube). Fill icing into paper or canvas bag and make a fine zig-zag pattern over the cookies.

Raisin cookies
120 cookies

1 stick (125 g) butter
¾ cup (2 dl) (confectioner's) sugar
2 eggs
¾ cup (2 dl) flour
⅔ cup (1½ dl) finely chopped raisins
3 tbsp brandy, rum, unflavored aquavit or vodka

Pour brandy over raisins and let them marinate for 1 hour. Preheat oven to 375—400°. Cream butter and sugar until the mixture is light and foamy. Add egg and flour, then add raisins and their liquid. Drop cookies (using two teaspoons) about the size of a nickel on well greased cookie sheets. Space them generously. Cook for 8—10 minutes. Remove from cookie sheets while they're still hot and cool.

cookies can now be bought at the supermarket it would be hard to imagine a big holiday without at least one or two home-made varieties. Today Scandinavian cookies are also available in the U.S.

Finnish cookies

50 cookies

6—7 oz (200 g) butter
⅓ cup (1 dl) sugar
2 oz (1 dl) grated almonds
1⅔ cup (4 dl) flour
½ tsp almond flavoring
1 egg
3—4 tbsp sugar
3—4 tbsp chopped almonds

Work butter until soft. Stir in sugar, grated almonds, almond flavoring and flour; form into a ball. Chill dough for 1 hour. Preheat oven to 350°. Roll dough into rolls ⅓—½" (1.5 cm) thick and cut them into 2" (5 cm) long cookies. Brush with beaten egg and sprinkle with sugar and chopped almonds. Cook on greased cookie sheets for 6—8 minutes or until golden colored.

Cookies from Uppåkra

50 cookies

1⅔ cup (4 dl) flour
⅓ cup (1 dl) cornstarch or potato flour
⅓ cup (1 dl) sugar
6—7 oz (200 g) butter
1 egg white
3—4 tbsp sugar
3—4 tbsp chopped almonds

Mix flour and sugar and cut in butter. Form a smooth ball. Chill dough until firm. Preheat oven to 350°. Roll out dough ⅛" (3 mm) thick. Cut round cookies, 2—2½" (5—6 cm) in diameter. Fold off-center so that the lower edge is showing. Brush with egg white and sprinkle with sugar and almonds. Cook on greased cookie sheets for 8—10 minutes. The cookies can also be filled with jam, usually raspberry preserve is used.

Scandinavian cookies are never very sweet—contrary to most American pastries and cakes. They are also light, brittle and often very pretty to look at. Americans add an amount of salt to their pastries

Grandmother's hearts
50 cookies

This is a good not too sweet old-fashioned cookie. If you don't have a heart-shaped cookie cutter, you can cut cookies with a medium-sized glass instead.

1¾ stick (200 g) butter
⅓ cup (1 dl) sugar
2 cups (5 dl) flour
1 egg yolk

Brush with:
egg white

Sprinkle with:
cinnamon and sugar

Mix flour and sugar and cut in butter, as if you were making a pie dough. Add egg yolk and gather dough into a ball. Chill for several hours. Preheat oven to 300—350°. Roll out dough on floured board until it is ¹/₈″ (3 mm) thick. Using a cookie cutter make hearts and put on well greased cookie sheets. Brush with lightly beaten egg white and sprinkle with cinnamon and sugar. Cook for 10—12 minutes.

Vanilla rings
50 cookies

1¾—2 cups (4½—5 dl) flour
⅓ cup (¾ dl) sugar
1 tbsp vanilla
6—7 oz (200 g) butter
1 egg yolk

Mix flour and sugar and cut in butter. Add egg yolk and vanilla and gather dough into a ball. Cool in refrigerator for 30 minutes. Preheat oven to 350°. Grease a cookie sheet. Force dough through a pastry bag with a wide notched metal tip and make round cookies directly on the cookie sheet. Cook for 10 minutes or until golden brown.

which seems excessive to a Scandinavian palate. On the contrary, for really superb cookies, the Scandinavian housewife would buy unsalted butter. In previous generations when women mostly stayed at

Danish apple cookies
20 double cookies

1¾ stick (200 g) butter
1 egg
⅔ cup (1½ dl) sugar
1½ tsp baking powder
2½ cup (6 dl) flour
tart apple sauce

Preheat oven to 425°. Cream butter, add egg and sugar. Sift flour with baking powder and add to butter mixture. Roll out dough about ⅛" (3 mm) thick, cut round cookies with cookie cutter or glass. Place on greased cookie sheets and cook for 6 minutes or until done. Cool. Spread half the cookies with tart apple sauce, put the other cookies on top as though you were making sandwiches. Sprinkle with confectioner's sugar.

Farmer's cookies
60 cookies

2½ cup (6 dl) flour
1 tsp baking soda
¾ cup (2 dl) sugar
2 tbsp syrup
⅓ cup (1 dl) chopped almonds
1¾ stick (200 g) butter

Mix flour with baking soda, sugar and almonds. Cut in butter, add syrup and gather into a dough. Knead for a few minutes, divide into three parts, and roll into rolls, 1½—2" (4—5 cm) in diameter. Chill. Preheat oven to 375—400°. Slice rolls into cookies about ¼" (6 mm) thick. Place on greased cookie sheets and cook for 8 minutes.

home and had help in the kitchen, tins filled with home-made cookies lined the pantry shelves. Two or three kinds were served each day for coffee at 11 a.m., or for an afternoon snack or a Sunday party.

Pancake cookies
35 cookies

1½ stick (200 g) butter
⅔ cup (1½ dl) sugar
2 eggs
¾ cup (2 dl) flour

To top with:
½ cup (1 dl) of a mixture of chopped almonds
   and sugar

Preheat oven to 425°. Melt butter and let
cool. Cream the melted butter until it is light
and foamy. Add sugar and eggs. Stir in flour.
Drop cookies, about the size of a teaspoon,
on greased cookie sheets, leaving room for
them to expand. Cook for about 5 minutes.
Remove cookie sheet from oven and quickly
sprinkle almond and sugar mixture on cookies. Return to oven and cook for another
5 minutes. Cookies can be shaped, "curled",
over a rolling pin or bottle while they are
still warm.

Norwegian custard cakes
24 pastries

1¼ cup (3 dl) flour
⅓ cup (1 dl) sugar
1⅔ stick (200 g) butter

Filling:
approximately 2 cups (5 dl) vanilla custard,
   see page 66

Mix flour and sugar and cut in butter.
Gather dough into a ball and chill for 1 hour.
Preheat oven to 400°. Butter 24 individual
muffin cups or small pastry pans. (In Norway they use heart-shaped pastry cups—nice
if you can find them.) Roll out ⅔ of dough,
line cups, fill with about 1 tbsp of vanilla
custard. Roll out remaining dough and place
top crusts on each pastry. Press down the
edges. Cook for 20 minutes or until done.
Let cool for a few minutes, then unmold
carefully. Serve cold, sprinkled with confectioner's sugar.

As soon as a tin was empty, a new batch was made
up. A grandmother kept a hand-written collection
of recipes; a new maid might bring one or two new
varieties into the house; an aunt left her favorite

Lace cookies
25 cookies

3 eggs
2 tbsp sugar
¾ cup (1¾ dl) table cream
1½ cup (3½ dl) flour
2 tbsp grated lemon rind
sugar to sprinkle them with
oil or shortening for deep fat frying

Beat eggs until light and foamy, add sugar
and beat for another couple of minutes.
Fold in cream, flour and grated lemon rind.
Heat fat for deep fat frying to 400° (210°C).
Use a pastry bag and squeeze lacy cookies
into the hot fat. Try to get the cookies as
round as possible and about 3″ (8 cm) in
diameter. Cook golden brown, remove and
drain on paper towel. Sprinkle with sugar
before serving.

Jenny's favorites
50 cookies

1⅔ stick (200 g) butter
⅔ cup (1½ dl) Quaker oats
⅔ cup (1½ dl) sugar
1 egg
1½ tsp baking powder
1 cup (2½ dl) flour

Frosting:
⅔ stick (75 g) butter
⅓ cup (1 dl) sugar
2 tbsp honey
½ cup (1¼ dl) almonds

Preheat oven to 300—350°. Melt butter for
cookies and pour it hot over oats. Add sugar
and egg. Sift flour and baking powder and
mix into butter and oat mixture. Chop almonds for frosting. Mix sugar, butter and
honey in a small pan and heat until sugar and
butter are completely dissolved. Remove
from heat and add almonds. Make cookies by
dropping batter on greased cookie sheets
with a teaspoon. Give them lots of room,
they expand to large, flat cookies. Cook for
5 minutes. Remove cookie sheets from oven
and drop about 1 teaspoon of frosting on
each cookie. Cook for another 6 minutes or
until golden brown and done.

recipes to her favorite niece. Recipes were tried,
changed and exchanged, and over the years many of
them have kept their old names: Jenny's favorites,
Grandmother's hearts, Miss Pihlgren's pretzels . . .

Ambrosia cake

2 eggs
⅔ cup (1½ dl) sugar
4 oz (125 g) butter
⅔ cup (1½ dl) flour

Icing:
¾ cup (2 dl) confectioner's sugar
2 tbsp water
1 tsp lemon juice
4 tbsp chopped, candied orange peel

Preheat oven to 400°. Beat eggs and sugar
until foamy. Melt butter and stir into egg
mixture. Add flour. Pour batter into buttered
cake pan and cook for about 30 minutes.
Stir confectioner's sugar and lemon juice
until smooth. Spread evenly over cold cake
and sprinkle with orange peel.

Tosca torte

2 eggs
⅔ cup (1½ dl) sugar
¾ cup (2 dl) flour
1 tsp baking powder
2 tbsp table cream
1 stick (125 g) butter

Frosting:
½ stick (60 g) butter
⅓ cup (1 dl) almonds
3 tbsp sugar
1 tbsp flour
1 tbsp table cream

Preheat oven to 325°. Beat eggs and sugar
until the mixture is light and foamy. Sift
flour with baking powder and add to egg
mixture. Melt butter over low heat and let
cool. Add cream and melted butter to batter.
Butter and flour (or bread) a round cake
form or frying pan with high boards. Pour
batter into pan and cook until it is half-done,
about 15—20 minutes.

Meanwhile chop almonds. Combine all ingredients for frosting in a small pan, stirring
constantly. Heat until butter is melted and
surface begins to bubble. Pour this mixture
over the half-done cake and continue cooking
it until it is done, another 15—20 minutes.
Total cooking time: about 40 minutes.

In a today's household where the wife is not employed
in a profession one can be sure to find home-made
buns and a sponge cake every Friday. One can still
hear housewives with small children saying: "I want

Tosca torte

my children to grow up remembering the smell of home-baked bread from mother's kitchen". There are nowadays so many factors which make it much easier to bake at home such as for example dried yeast.

Sugar cake

This is the classic Scandinavian cake recipe; it's a basic recipe to which you can add vanilla, grated lemon or orange rind and juice, 1½ tbsp cocoa, almond flavoring, etc. Sliced sugar cake is served with coffee, or with a glass of milk or juice. Slices topped with fruit and whipped cream are often served for dessert. Sliced horizontally and filled with custard or fruit and topped with whipped cream, it becomes the classic Scandinavian torte, which is served as a Sunday dessert or for some special occasion.

3 eggs
¾ cup (2 dl) sugar
1 cup (3 dl) flour
1½ tsp baking powder
3 oz (90 g) melted butter

Preheat oven to 350°. Beat eggs and sugar until foamy. Mix flour and baking powder and add to egg mixture. Melt butter and stir into batter. Pour into buttered and floured cake pan and cook for about 50 minutes or until done.

Almond sugar cake

¾ cup (2 dl) almonds
5 oz (150 g) butter
1 cup (2½ dl) sugar
3 eggs
1 cup (2½ dl) flour
1 tsp baking powder

Preheat oven to 350°. Beat butter and sugar until light and foamy. Add one egg at a time, beating batter in between. Add grated almonds. Mix flour and baking powder and stir into batter. Pour into greased and floured baking pan and cook for about 50 minutes.

You can always keep dried yeast at home and that makes it easy to bake some buns when you feel like doing it. A lot of coffee is consumed in Scandinavia. Sweden is the leading coffee consuming country in

Jelly roll
20 slices

3 eggs
⅔ cup (1½ dl) sugar
¾ cup (2 dl) flour
1 tsp baking powder

Filling:
¾ cup (2 dl) tart jam, apple sauce or sugared,
    mashed berries, or the same amount of
    your favorite cream or custard filling

Preheat oven to 450°. Beat eggs and sugar
light and foamy. Mix flour and baking powder and add to batter. Beat until smooth.
Grease a shallow baking pan, about 12 ×
16 × 1″ (30 × 40 cm). Pour batter into pan
and cook for 5 minutes. Sprinkle cake with
sugar. Loosen the edges and reverse on foil or
wax paper that has been dusted with sugar.
Spread jam on top and roll cake. Keep in
paper or foil until cold and ready to serve.

Spice cake

2 eggs
⅔ cup (1½ dl) sugar
2 tsp cinnamon
1 tsp ginger
1 tsp cloves
1¼ cup (3 dl) flour
2 tsp baking powder
3 oz (90 g) butter
⅔ cup (1½ dl) sour cream

Preheat oven to 350°. Beat eggs and sugar
until light and foamy. Stir in spices. Mix
flour and baking powder and add to egg
mixture. Melt butter and blend into batter
together with sour cream. Pour into greased
and floured (or breaded) baking pan and
cook for 45 minutes or until done.

Europe. And with the coffee you, of course, like
to have a cookie. By tradition one bakes a lot of
cookies at home. The Scandinavian housewives are
pretty economical, and there is no doubt that there

Layer cake from Finland

This recipe, which is traditionally Finnish, may seem odd at first glance; it contains no sugar. But the torte is delicious, the cakes slightly crunchy and very light. Tart apple sauce or a good tart jelly gives it its flavor. The whipped cream topping can be sweetened with confectioner's sugar.

equal weight butter, flour and grated, boiled potatoes; 5 oz (150 g) of each will make a cake that's sufficient for 6 people
5 oz (150 g) butter
5 oz (150 g) flour (⅔ cup—1½ dl)
5 oz (150 g) boiled, peeled and grated potatoes

Preheat oven to 425°. Cut butter and potatoes into the flour and gather dough into a ball. Divide the dough into four even parts and roll each part into a round cake, ¹/₈″ (3 mm) thick. The dough can be rolled between pieces of wax paper; remove the top paper and transfer the lower one directly onto a cookie sheet and into the oven. Prick the cakes with a fork and cook for about 10 minutes. Let cool. Layer the cakes with filling of tart apple sauce or jelly and cover with whipped cream. Serve cool.

Sun cake

3 eggs
1 cup (2½ dl) sugar
1 cup (2½ dl) flour
1 tsp baking powder
5 oz (150 g) butter
½ cup (1 dl) almonds

Preheat oven to 350°. Beat eggs and sugar until foamy. Mix flour and baking powder and add to egg mixture. Melt butter and stir into batter. Pour into buttered and floured cake pan. Chop and split almonds into halves. Sprinkle almonds over cake and cook for about 40 minutes.

is a lot of pennies to be saved by baking yourself. Also when it comes to cookies and cakes there are a lot of semi-manufactured products. There are the complete mixers and also the deep frozen products

Royal potato cake

3 oz (90 g) butter
¾ cup (2 dl) sugar
3 eggs
3½ oz (100 g) boiled, cold potatoes (2 medium-sized potatoes)
2 tsp cream of wheat
⅔ cup (1½ dl) almonds

Preheat oven to 350°. Grate potatoes or put through a blender. Beat sugar and butter till light and foamy. Add egg yolks and grated potatoes, together with grated or finely chopped almonds. Beat egg whites until stiff and fold into batter together with cream of wheat. Pour batter into well greased and floured (or breaded) round cake pan and cook for 20—30 minutes or until done. Let cool for 10 minutes before reversing it on a platter. Dust with confectioner's sugar. Can be served warm together with cold whipped cream, with vanilla or lemon custard, or with ice cream.

Cardamon muffins
20 muffins

½ stick (60 g) butter
1 egg
⅔ cup (1½ dl) sugar
⅓ cup (1 dl) table cream
1 tsp baking powder
1—2 tsp ground cardamon
¾ cup (2 dl) flour

Preheat oven to 300—350°. Melt butter and let it cool. Beat egg and sugar until the mixture is foamy. Sift or mix flour with baking powder and cardamon. Add half this mixture to egg and sugar. Add cream. Blend in remaining flour, then carefully add cool butter. Fill batter to ⅔ in buttered and floured muffin tins. Cook for 12—15 minutes. Let cool a few minutes, then remove from tins. The muffins are best while they're still warm, but they contain so much moisture that they can also be reheated.

to facilitate the baking. The most common though is to do the whole job yourself and to make big batches and then put them in the freezer. Before Christmas you can find many recipes for home-baked

Puff pastry torte

This torte is made from the classic flaky or puff pastry. It's not easy to make: the butter tends to melt before you've finished rolling out the dough, and the cake often rises more on one side than on the other. Don't attempt it on a hot summer day. But if you have some cooking experience, can work fast, and own a reliable oven with an even temperature, you should succeed. It's worth the trouble. The dough can be used for a wide variety of other cookies and cakes. There are many ways to prepare puff pastry; if you've got a favorite recipe, use it for this torte.

Puff pastry:
1½ cup (3½ dl) flour
⅔ cup (1½ dl) water
2 sticks (250 g) butter

Chill butter in refrigerator. Mix flour and water, gather into a ball, and knead lightly until smooth. The process shouldn't take more than a few minutes. Chill dough in refrigerator. The dough and the butter should both be cold.

Roll the dough into a neat rectangle about ¼″ (6 mm) thick; roll as evenly as possible and make the edges of the dough as even as you can. Slice the chilled butter and put it on half the dough, about 1″ (2.5 cm) from the edges, fold the other half over and seal the sides by pressing down with your fingers.

Give the dough a quarter turn and roll into another neat rectangle the size of the first one. Fold dough into three exactly even parts and press down the edges. Give the dough another quarter turn, roll it out again, and again fold it into three even parts. Repeat this process four times in all. Once the dough has been rolled and folded a few times it becomes transparent; the butter shows through the thin layers of dough. The dough should not break and the butter should not melt. You have to work rather fast and in a cool kitchen. Wrap the dough in foil and chill for 30 minutes.

Preheat oven to 425°. Divide dough into 5 equal parts, and roll each part into a round cake. Keep whatever dough you're not working with in the refrigerator so it stays cold. Prick each cake with a fork and brush with cold water. Place on cold cookie sheets rinsed with cold water. Cook for 10 minutes. Cool cakes and stack them, using whipped cream and fresh sliced strawberries, tart apple sauce, or any kind of custard, as layering.

cookies and cakes in the weekly magazines. The ambitious housewife, and most of the Scandinavian housewives are still very ambitious, bake big batches and freeze them to save for the many parties

Kinuski torte

Very light sugar cake:
4 eggs
¾ cup (2 dl) sugar
⅓ cup (1 dl) flour
1 tsp baking powder
3 tbsp potato flour or cornstarch

Vanilla custard:
1¼ cup (3 dl) table cream
2 egg yolks
2 tbsp sugar
1 tbsp cornstarch
2—3 tsp vanilla

Kinuski topping:
2 cups (5 dl) table cream
1 cup (2½ dl) sugar
⅓ cup (1 dl) light syrup
3 tbsp butter
1 tsp vanilla

Preheat oven to 400°. Beat eggs and sugar until white and foamy. Mix flour and cornstarch with baking powder and add to egg mixture. Pour into greased and floured round cake pan and cook for 30 minutes or until done. Let cool. Cut into three layers and fill with vanilla custard and tart apple sauce.

Combine cream, egg yolks, sugar and cornstarch in top of double boiler. Beat constantly and simmer until mixture has thickened. Let cool and stir from time to time so that the custard is smooth. Add vanilla to taste.

Combine cream, sugar and syrup and simmer gently over low heat till sheeting stage (220°), or until a few drops of the mixture form a soft ball when dropped in cold water. Add butter and vanilla. Pour hot over cake and let cool.

of the Christmas holidays. One can hardly find such a busy housewife that she doesn't have time to bake at least three or four kinds of cookies for the Christmas holidays. One or two cakes goes without saying.

Sweet yeast bread

In Scandinavia there is a wide variety of sweet
yeast bread. If the coffee break isn't accompanied
by a cookie you often get a slice of sweet yeast
bread or a bun of a similar dough. A bun and a

Sweet yeast bread
48 small buns or 3—5 loaves

The basic ingredients are simple: ordinary, not self-rising flour, yeast, sugar, milk, and margarine or butter (shortening is unknown in Scandinavia). But there is a wealth of different recipes. For special occasions the buns or yeast breads can become quite elaborate. They may contain eggs, lots of butter, raisins, cardamon, cinnamon, candied fruit or orange peel, cream instead of milk, and even saffron.

If you've never made yeast bread, it may seem like an awesome undertaking. Actually it's quite easy. There are two kinds of yeast: fresh (or compressed) yeast, and dry powdered yeast. Fresh yeast comes in cakes and should be dissolved in liquid that's about 85°. Powdered yeast requires a temperature of 110—115° for dissolving. If the liquid is too hot the yeast bacteria will die; if it's too cold the yeast won't dissolve.

Yeast bread doesn't rise immediately: it takes time for the yeast bacteria to multiply. It can take anywhere from 40 minutes to 2 hours, depending on the temperature of the room: the higher the temperature the faster the dough will rise. If the room where you are working is cool, you can place the bowl containing your dough into a larger bowl filled with warm water. Yeast dough rises more rapidly at high altitudes and has to be watched carefully.

2 oz (60 g) yeast
2 cups (5 dl) milk
1 stick (125 g) butter
⅓ cup (1 dl) sugar
2 tsp ground cardamon
(1 egg)
5½—6 cups (1½ l) flour
1 egg to brush them with

Sprinkle with:
sugar (and chopped almonds)

Melt butter over low heat. Add milk and heat to 85°. Crumble yeast in a large bowl. Pour lukewarm milk over yeast and stir until it is completely dissolved. Add sugar, cardamon and 4 cups (1 l) flour. Now (add egg and) gradually work in another cup (2½ dl) of flour. Work dough until it begins to leave the sides of the bowl. Sprinkle a few tablespoons of flour on top of dough, cover bowl with a towel and let rise until it is double in size — 40 minutes to 1 hour.

Punch down dough with a wooden spoon and knead on a floured board until it is smooth and shiny — about 5 minutes. Shape into buns, loaves etc. Let rise again until the buns or loaves have doubled in bulk. Brush with lightly beaten egg and sprinkle with sugar and almonds. Cook loaves for 20 minutes at 375—400°. Cook buns at 475—500° for 5 minutes.

glass of milk is what children get as an after-school snack. Sweet yeast bread is taken along for picnics and outings. It is served with coffee or tea, and is often eaten as a late evening snack

Cinnamon buns
50 buns

Prepare dough according to recipe on page 93

Filling:
1 stick (125 g) butter
⅔ cup (1½ dl) sugar
2—3 tbsp cinnamon

Brush with:
1 egg

Preheat oven to 475—500°. When dough has risen once, punch it down, turn it out on a floured board and knead it a few times. Roll out half the dough at a time to a rectangle, ⅛—¼" (½ cm) thick. Spread with butter, sprinkle with sugar and cinnamon and roll it into a roll. Cut slices, about 1" (2.5 cm) thick and put them into paper cups, cut side up. Let rise on cookie sheets, brush with beaten egg and bake for 7 minutes or until nicely browned.

Yeast bread with apples

½ batch yeast dough, see recipe page 93
5 medium-sized tart apples
1 lemon
1 tbsp cinnamon
⅓ cup (1 dl) sugar
⅓ cup (1 dl) chopped almonds
or 6 oz (200 g) almond paste

Preheat oven to 375—400°. Prepare yeast dough. Roll it and put it into a buttered shallow baking dish. Peel and pare apples, cut them into thin slices and arrange them on top of the dough. Sprinkle with lemon juice, cinnamon, sugar and almonds, or with grated or chopped almond paste. Cook for 25 minutes.

with yet another cup of tea. At Christmas, and then especially for the feast of St Lucie on December 13 the sweet yeast bread is flavored with saffron and buns are made in different traditional shapes.

Lenten buns

10 buns

These large buns are made only during the weeks before Easter. They're cut in halves and put together again with a filling of whipped cream and almond paste and eaten on a soup plate together with hot milk and cinnamon. If this seems too exotic to you, the yeast dough recipe is a particularly good one: you can make smaller lenten buns, fill them and eat them for dessert with a cup of coffee.

2 oz (60 g) yeast
¾ cup (2 dl) table cream
1 stick (125 g) butter
4 tbsp sugar
1 tsp ground cardamon
½ tsp almond flavoring
1 egg
3 cups (¾ l) flour

Brush with:
1 egg

Preheat oven to 475—500°. Crumble yeast in large mixing bowl. Melt butter over low heat, add cream and heat mixture till 85°. Pour over yeast and stir until it is completely dissolved. Add sugar, cardamon, almond flavoring, egg and about half the flour.

Beat the dough, adding remaining flour a little at a time. (Reserve a few tablespoons of flour to flour the board.) The dough should be smooth and begin to leave the sides of the bowl. Sprinkle a tablespoon of flour over the dough, cover it with a towel and let rise until it has doubled in bulk, 40 minutes to 2 hours.

Punch down dough, then knead it on a floured board until it is very smooth. Shape it into ten large (or more smaller) buns. Put them on greased cookie sheets and let them rise till double size. Brush with lightly beaten egg. Cook for 8—10 minutes.

In the latest years home-baking has become very popular in Scandinavia as well as in the U.S. The most households have an electric mixer which helps to mix the dough. It is good to eat home-made bread

Danish pastry

32 pastries

Danish pastry is not easy to make. Unless you are used to handling a soft dough and can work fast, you may not get the wonderfully flaky pastries but something a bit harder and more dry. Danish pastry is made from a yeast dough, into which butter or margarine or shortening is rolled, exactly as if you were making puff pastry. But it's harder to make than puff pastry, because the dough you're working with tends to rise while you're handling it. It is essential to work in a cool kitchen—nothing for a hot summer day.

Dough:
1⅛ oz (50 g) yeast
a pinch of salt
2 tbsp sugar
1 egg
½ cup (1¼ dl) milk
2 cups (5 dl) flour

To roll into the dough:
1 stick (125 g) cold butter

Filling I:
Vanilla custard, see page 66.

Filling II:
Almond paste; the paste should be semi-soft: if it is too hard you can grate it (or put it through a blender) and mix in 1 egg white

Filling III:
Any good, tart jelly or jam

To brush pastries:
1 egg

To make the dough: Crumble yeast into a large mixing bowl. Add salt and sugar, and stir until the yeast is dissolved. Beat egg lightly with the milk and add to the yeast. Gradually stir in flour to a smooth rather firm dough. Roll out dough to a rectangle, about ½" (1.5 cm) thick. Work fast so that the dough doesn't start rising. Now roll in butter. Slice chilled butter into thin slices and put it on half the dough, about ½—1" (2—2.5 cm) from the edges. Fold the other half over, seal, turn the dough and roll out again exactly as if you were making puff pastry, see details page 90. If the dough starts rising before you're finished rolling and folding it, you can chill it for 30 minutes or more and then start working it again. Chill dough for at least 1 hour before shaping it into pastries.

Preheat oven to 500°. For different shapes of pastries, and how to fill them, see pictures beside. Put pastries on greased cookie sheets and let rise. Brush with lightly beaten egg. Cook for 10 minutes.

and there is a common discussion about the additives in industrial made bread. Especially young people are very engaged in the nutrition debate and like to know what they are eating. Flour and other

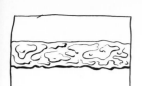

Combs

Whole wheat bread
1 bread

1⅓ oz (2 cakes compressed) (40 g) yeast
1¼ cup (3 dl) milk
½ stick (60 g) butter
1 tsp salt
2 tbsp syrup
2⅓ cup (6 dl) whole wheat flour
1½ cup (3½ dl) all purpose flour

Crumble yeast in a large bowl and dissolve in a few tablespoons of cold milk. Melt butter over low heat. Remove from heat and add remaining milk. Now pour this lukewarm mixture into the bowl. Add salt, syrup and whole wheat flour. Gradually add all purpose flour. Beat dough until it is smooth and begins to leave the sides of the bowl. Sprinkle about 1 tablespoon flour on top, cover and let rise until it has doubled in bulk, 30 minutes to 1 hour, depending on the temperature of the room.

Preheat oven to 400°. Grease a loaf pan. Punch down dough, turn it out onto a lightly floured board and knead it until it is smooth. Roll it into an even loaf and put it in the pan. Let rise until it has doubled in bulk. Cook for 40 minutes or until done. Brush the hot bread quickly with cold water. Let it cool a few minutes, remove it from the pan, wrap it in a kitchen towel and let it cool.

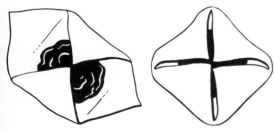

Spandau

ingredients for the bread are often purchased in health food stores. In young families it is very common that the man does the baking. Many young men of today are interested in cooking. They find it

Farm bread
2 breads

*Traditional Swedish bread often contains
sugar or syrup, sometimes even raisins,
orange peel and spices like fennel or anis
seeds which many other cuisines associate
with desserts. However, Americans are used
to slightly sweetened breads for sandwiches,
and this sweet, rather heavy rye bread tastes
very good with a strong (Scandinavian)
cheese.*

1½ cup (3½ dl) milk
⅔ cup (1½ dl) syrup
⅔ oz (1 cake compressed yeast) (20 g)
1 tsp salt
⅔ cup (1½ dl) rye flour
3 cups (7½ dl) all purpose flour

Brush with:
⅓ cup (1 dl) water
1 tsp syrup

Slowly heat milk and syrup to 85°. Remove
about ½ cup (1 dl) of this mixture and
dissolve yeast in the lukewarm liquid. Pour
yeast and remaining milk mixture into a
large bowl. Add salt, rye flour and about half
of the all purpose flour. Beat the dough until
it is smooth and begins to leave the sides of
the bowl. Cover the bowl with a kitchen
towel or paper towel and let the dough rise
until it has doubled in bulk, 40 minutes to
1 hour. (See also detailed instructions,
page 93, Sweet yeast bread.)

Punch down the dough, turn it out onto a
lightly floured board and knead in the remaining flour. Preheat oven to 375—400°.
Grease two loaf pans lightly. Knead dough,
divide it in halves and shape each half into an
even loaf. Place loaves in buttered pans and
let them rise until they have doubled in bulk,
about 30 minutes to 1 hour. Mix water and
syrup and brush loaves with this mixture.
Cook for about 1 hour or until done.

nice to work with their hands and to be interested
in cooking is very up-to-date nowadays. Bread has
always been very important in the Scandinavian diet.
At every meal you will find many different types

Swedish rye bread

4 breads

This bread is traditionally made into round cakes, about 5″ (12 cm) in diameter. For a great Scandinavian sandwich, slice the cakes lengthwise, spread with butter and decorate one fourth with cheese and radishes; one fourth with ham together with pickles; one fourth with sliced hard-boiled eggs and Swedish anchovies or a piece of matjes herring and a sprig of dill, and the remaining fourth with cold meatballs or a generous slice of liverwurst, relish and parsley.

2 cakes compressed (1⅓ oz) (40 g) yeast
½ stick (60 g) butter
2 cups (5 dl) milk
1 tsp salt
⅓ cup (1 dl) syrup
1 tbsp anis seeds or fennel
2 cups (5 dl) rye flour
3½ — 4 cups (8½ dl—1 l) all purpose flour

Crumble cakes of yeast in a large bowl. Melt butter over low heat and add milk. Remove from heat and pour it over yeast. Stir until yeast is completely dissolved. Add salt, syrup and spice and half the rye flour. Gradually add the remaining rye flour and the all purpose flour. Beat dough until it is smooth and begins to leave the sides of the bowl. Sprinkle a tablespoon all purpose flour over the dough, cover it, and let rise until it has doubled in bulk, 40 minutes to 1 hour.

Punch down dough, turn it out onto a floured board and divide it into fourths. Knead each fourth well until it is smooth and elastic, gather it into a ball and roll into a round cake. Preheat oven to 425°. Put cakes on greased cookie sheets and let them rise until they have doubled in bulk. Prick them lightly with a fork and cook for 10 minutes or until they are done. Brush hot cakes with water.

of bread as for example rye bread, farm bread, whole wheat bread and, of course, the traditional Scandinavian crisp bread. Nowadays Scandinavian crisp bread can be bought almost in every Western country.

The traditional Christmas table

Christmas

Liver paté

1 lb (500 g) pork liver
½ lb (250 g) fat back
1 red onion
6 fillets of Scandinavian anchovies
1 tsp ground cloves
1 tsp ground black pepper
1 tbsp salt
2 eggs
3 tbsp butter
3 tbsp flour
1⅔ cup (4 dl) milk

Preheat oven to 400°. Grind liver and fat back finely, together with onion and fillets of anchovies. Mix in lightly beaten egg yolks and spices. Melt butter over low heat and blend in flour. Slowly stir in milk. Cook and stir until thickened and smooth. Cool. Stir into liver mixture. Whip egg whites stiff and carefully fold into mixture. Pour into well greased loaf pan, set the pan into a larger one of hot water and cook for about 1 hour or until done.

Scrapple

4 lb (2 kg) veal shank, neck or breast
8 cups (2 l) water
1 tbsp salt
½ tbsp whole pepper
1 tsp whole allspice
1 bay leaf
2 whole cloves
1 onion

To season scrapple:
salt
pepper
pickling vinegar
2 tbsp gelatin

Put meat in a large pot and add water, spices and sliced onion. Boil until quite tender. Strain, reserving liquid. Cut meat from bones and cut into small pieces or grind it coarsely. Strain stock once more, add meat and heat. Season well with salt, pepper and pickling vinegar. Dissolve gelatin in a few tablespoons of cold water and stir into meat mixture. Pour into one large or several small molds and chill.

Christmas is a big holiday in Scandinavia, even bigger and more important than in America. Food is prepared weeks in advance. Houses are cleaned until they shine. There is a smell of gingerbread

Headcheese

Headcheese is an old-fashioned dish. It's usually made either from hog's head or calf's head mixed together with fresh ham or other lean uncured pork, and with veal breast, shoulder or shank. Larger American cookbooks contain detailed recipes for preparing a head. If you don't want to try handling a calf's or hog's head you can still enjoy this traditional Scandinavian Christmas dish: the recipe given below uses other cuts of meat, omitting the head.

**5 lb (2½ kg) pork shoulder butt or fresh
    pic-nic
2—2½ lb (1 kg) veal breast, shoulder or
    shank
1 large piece of fresh pork rind**

**For every quart (liter) of water use:
1 tbsp salt
5 grains of pepper
5 grains of allspice
2 cloves
½ bay leaf
½ carrot
a few slices of onion**

**For the mold:
cotton cloth or towel
thin slices of fat back
2 tbsp gelatin
2 tbsp salt
1 tsp coarsely ground pepper
1 tsp coarsely ground allspice
½ tsp ground cloves**

Cover meat with cold water. Let boil, skim, then add spices, carrot and onion. Cover and simmer until very tender, about 2 hours. Strain and reserve stock. Cut meat from bones and cut into thin slices. Wring cloth in hot water and line a deep bowl. Line cloth with thin strips of fat back. Arrange fat and lean meat in alternate layers. Sprinkle spices in between and a little bit of gelatin. Cover with strips of fat back. Pull cloth together tightly and secure with a string. Place bundle in a pan and cover with stock. Simmer for 15 minutes.

Remove headcheese to a large plate. Cover with weighted board and cool in cloth for 24 hours. Headcheese will keep in brine. To make brine, boil 1 quart (1 l) of water with ⅓ cup (1 dl) salt (coarse or kosher salt if possible) and 1 tbsp sugar. Cool before using. Headcheese is served cold in thin slices with pickled beets.

and "glögg", of buns and sausages, an atmosphere of anticipation. In Scandinavia, people begin to looking forward to Christmas as early as November, when the light begins to wane and the days shorten.

Christmas sausage

3 lb (1½ kg) lean pork
1 lb (500 g) fat back
1 tbsp salt
½ —1 tbsp ground pepper
1 tsp ground allspice
1 tsp ground ginger
4 cups (1 l) pork or beef stock
⅓ cup (1 dl) cornstarch or ½ lb (250 g)
    boiled ground potatoes
about 7 feet casing

Curing:
4 tbsp salt
2 tbsp sugar
½ tbsp saltpeter (hard to find, it's used only
    to give the sausage a better color)

Grind pork and fat back finely. Add spices,
cornstarch or potatoes, and stock. Check
consistency by dropping a tablespoon of the
mixture into boiling water: if it doesn't
hold together, you need more cornstarch.
Cut casing into 15″ (38 cm) pieces. Tie one
end securely. Fill loosely and tie other end
(it's impossible to fill the casing without a
special attachment on your meat grinder).
Rinse sausages in cold water. Dry them,
rub with the curing mixture, and chill over
night.

The sausage will keep in the refrigerator for
a few days; to be kept longer it has to be
frozen or put in brine, see page 102. To serve:
place sausage in enough cold water to cover.
Simmer slowly, uncovered, for about 30 minutes. Serve with mashed potatoes and mustard, or cut into slices and put on Christmas
smörgåsbord.

It is not yet cold, but the sky is often covered
and the darkness can become oppressive. Christmas
is something to dream about; decorated trees in
homes, yards and city streets, candle light, good

Herring salad
10 servings

4 fillets of salt herring
8 medium-sized boiled potatoes
2 large tart apples
6 pickled beets
1 onion
pepper
beet juice
(¾—1 cup (2—2½ dl) whipping cream)

Garnish:
2 hard-boiled eggs
parsley

Soak herring over night. Peel potatoes and apples. Cube all ingredients finely and mix together. Add beet juice and pepper to taste. (Medium stiff, whipped cream is sometimes added to the salad. It makes for a more mild, creamy taste.) Rinse a bowl with cold water and firm down salad. Chill for several hours, then unmold on a platter. Garnish with sliced hard-boiled eggs and parsley.

Pickled herring

The classic marinated herring, a must on every Scandinavian smörgåsbord and Christmas table.

4 fillets of salt herring
1 piece horse-radish, about 1″ (2.5 cm) long
1 carrot
2 red onions
2 bay leaves
2 tsp allspice
2 tsp mustard seeds
2 small pieces dried ginger or 1 tsp ground ginger

Marinade:
¾ cup (2 dl) pickling vinegar
⅔ cup (1½ dl) water
1 cup (2½ dl) sugar

Soak herring over night. Wash, drain and cut into 1″ (2—3 cm) pieces. Boil water, vinegar and sugar for marinade and cool. Peel horse-radish, carrot, and onions and cut into thin slices. Layer herring with onions, carrots, horse-radish and spices in a tall, wide-mouthed jar or crock. Cover the fish with marinade. Marinate in refrigerator for 1 day. Fresh horse-radish may be hard to find. A tablespoon of ready-made grated horse-radish can be sprinkled between the herring layers instead.

food, heady spices and companionship. It is the family feast above all other feasts. From far away the children are coming together with their families to celebrate Christmas in their parents home.

Pickled herring

The traditions around Christmas varies. What is common in one part of the country might not exist at all in another. What one does in east has often very little to do with the celebration in west.

Glazed Christmas ham

A Scandinavian Christmas ham is cured with sugar and salt, never smoked. Any uncooked American ham cured in brine can be served with the traditional Swedish glaze. Dry-cured hams (Virginia, Smithfield etc) are an American speciality and cannot be used in this recipe. The ham you buy at the supermarket most likely will not need any soaking. A Scandinavian butcher—if there is one in your home town—may cure his own hams and will tell you whether they have to be soaked before cooking.

1 ham, 7—12 lb (3—6 kg)

Glaze:
1 egg
2 tbsp mustard
1 tbsp sugar
3—4 tbsp unseasoned bread crumbs

Garnish:
store-bought or home-made white frosting,
or about ¾ stick (90 g) of creamed butter

Preheat oven to 325°. Place ham with skin side up on a rack over large pan. Put meat thermometer in the thickest, meatiest part, but so that it doesn't touch the bone.

The ham is done when its temperature is 170° (77°C), which takes about ½ hour per lb (500 g). Remove from oven, cool so that you can handle it easily and peel off skin. Let cool completely, possibly over night. Reserve drippings.

Preheat oven to 475°. Mix egg, sugar and mustard and spread over ham. Sift bread crumbs over. Put ham on rack over pan and bake for 8—10 minutes or until nicely brown. Traditionally the Swedish ham is served with a garnish of frosting or creamed butter. Use pastry bag with a fine tip. Garnish with roses or doodles around the edges and write in the middle: God Jul — Merry Christmas.

The Christmas holidays in Scandinavia are long. One celebrates Christmas Eve, Christmas Day and also the third day of Christmas. This gives everybody enough time to enjoy the great number of dishes.

Christmas dip

Chill ham drippings in refrigerator for a night and remove some of the fat. The remaining stock should have a strong taste; probably you can add some water. There should be at least 2 cups (5 dl) of liquid. Add other stock or the liquid you've boiled the Christmas sausage in, if there isn't enough. Season well with salt, a little soy sauce, possibly some finely crushed sage.

Simmer slowly and leave on the stove or put on warming candles or an electric tray on the Christmas table. Guests dip one or several pieces of bread (dark, rye, white, and the traditional "vörtbröd") in the stock and eat it together with slices of ham, spiced cabbage and boiled potatoes.

Christmas spareribs
6 servings

2—2½ lb (1 kg) country spareribs
1 tbsp ground ginger or dry mustard
1 tbsp salt
1 tsp ground pepper
1¼ cup (3 dl) stock

Preheat oven to 350°. Mix spices and rub into meat. Pour stock into a shallow baking pan. Put meat on rack in pan and bake uncovered for 1—1½ hours, or until done. No basting is necessary. Serve with cooked apple halves, filled with currant jelly, cooked prunes or with tart apple sauce.

In the middle of the morning of Christmas Eve relatives and friends are getting together for "a dip in the pot". That is a nice way to start the Christmas celebration. One dips rye bread

Danish spicy red cabbage

This is mainly Christmas food, to be served with glazed ham or spareribs. It tastes very good with pork roast, with sausage and even with turkey. Spicy red cabbage can be made weeks before Christmas and frozen. It freezes very well and is good reheated, though it may get a little bit more mushy in the process.

2—3 heads of red cabbage
2 onions
4 tart apples
¾ cup (2 dl) cider vinegar
½—1 cup (1—2 dl) brown sugar
lard, ham drippings or butter
6 cloves
1 bay leaf
3 grains of allspice
salt
**1—2 cups (3—4 dl) red wine or cranberry
  juice**

Shred cabbage. Peel and slice onions. Sauté in lard, ham drippings or butter, in heavy pot. Add cured, peeled and quartered apples and spices. Season with sugar and vinegar to taste and add enough red wine or cranberry juice to moisten cabbage thoroughly. Cover and simmer over low heat until cabbage is very tender, 1½ hours or more. Check seasoning. It's a matter of taste how spicy you want the cabbage.

Christmas porridge
4—5 servings

⅔ cup (1½ dl) rice
1¼ cup (3 dl) water
1 piece cinnamon
1 tbsp butter
3⅓—3½ cup (8 dl) milk
dash of salt
1 tbsp sugar

Boil water and butter. Add rice and cinnamon. Cover and simmer over low heat until water has evaporated. Add milk, cover and simmer over very low heat until rice is very tender, about 40 minutes. Stir porridge from time to time. Season with a dash of salt and some sugar.

The easiest way to make porridge is in a double boiler. Boil rice in water, add milk, then place in double boiler until done.
A single blanched almond is usually added to the porridge. Whoever gets the almond will marry the coming year, for sure. Serve porridge warm with milk, sugar and ground cinnamon.

flavored with worth in hot broth and enjoys it with the Christmas sausage. The lye-cured fish, lutfish, and the Christmas porridge are often served as the last meal on Christmas Eve's night.

Baked lutfish
4—5 servings

*Lutfish is dried ling, a variety of codfish,
which is lye-cured and then soaked in water
for several days. It's a Scandinavian specialty, a reminder of ancient customs. Lye-curing
was a way of preserving in the old days
when there were few ways to keep food.
The tradition of eating lutfish for Christmas
is a Catholic one. Even though the Scandinavian countries have officially been Protestant ever since the fifteen hundreds, lutfish is
still a Christmas tradition in the majority
of Scandinavian homes. Children are often
served Christmas porridge instead of Lutfish,
see recipe beside.*

*Lutfish tastes like nothing else. It's bland
and pungent at the same time: it has an
odd smell, not fishy, more like very ripe
Camembert. Lutfish can be bought at
Christmas time in Scandinavian speciality
stores.*

4 lb (2 kg) lutfish
2 tbsp salt
1 tbsp butter

Cream sauce:
4 tbsp butter
3 tbsp flour
2 cups (5 dl) table cream
salt
pepper

Preheat oven to 400°. Sprinkle fish with salt
and put it skin side down in a buttered
baking dish. Cover with aluminium foil and
bake for 30—40 minutes. Pour off water
before serving. Remove foil and serve with
melted butter and/or cream sauce, salt,
pepper, ground allspice, mustard, boiled
potatoes and sweet peas.

Melt butter over low heat and blend in flour.
Slowly stir in cream. Cook and stir over low
heat until thickened and smooth, about
5 minutes. Season. Add about 1 tbsp of cold
butter for better flavor.

By looking at the various ways of celebration
one can clearly see the difference in the Scandinavian peoples' habits. A Norwegian Christmas
is for example very different from a Danish one.

Christmas stars
30 cookies

2½ stick (300 g) butter
2½ cup (6 dl) flour
⅓ cup (1 dl) table cream

Filling:
8 oz (240 g) seedless prunes
⅓ cup (1 dl) sugar
⅓ cup (1 dl) chopped filberts or almonds

To brush with:
1 egg

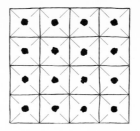

Christmas stars

Cut butter into flour, add cream and gather into a ball. Chill for 1 hour. Use the soft, seedless variety of prunes (other kinds will have to be soaked for several hours before they are ready to use). Chop them or put them through a blender. Add sugar and nuts.

Preheat oven to 500°. Roll out dough ⅛—¼″ (½ cm) thick. Cut squares with 2″ (5 cm) sides. Make a cut from each corner about 1″ (2.5 cm) deep diagonally towards the middle. Put a heaping teaspoon of filling in the middle. Fold as shown in picture. Beat egg lightly and brush cookies. Cook on greased cookie sheets 5—10 minutes.

Christmas stars can also be made of Puff pastry, see recipe page 90. Work then with half or a third of the dough at a time, keeping the remaining dough in the refrigerator.

The famous Swedish Christmas dinner-table for example, is considerably more luxurious than the Christmas dinner-tables in Finland and Norway. But these countries have now taken up some of the

Gingerbread cookies
150 cookies

2 sticks (250 g) butter
¾ cup (2 dl) sugar
⅔ cup (1½ dl) syrup
2—3 tbsp cinnamon
1 tsp ground cloves
1 tsp ground cardamon
1 tbsp ground ginger
1 cup (2½ dl) chopped almonds
1 tsp baking soda
4 cups (1 l) flour

Prepare dough a day in advance. Melt butter in large pan over low heat. Remove from heat. Add sugar, syrup, spices, baking soda, almonds and about 3½ cup (7 dl) of flour. Knead dough on floured board until it is smooth and gradually work in remaining flour. Roll dough into rolls, 2″ (5 cm) in diameter. Chill over night. Preheat oven to 350°. Slice rolls into thin cookies and put on greased cookie sheets. Cook for 10—12 minutes.

Almond tarts
35 tarts

⅔ cup (1½ dl) butter
⅓ cup (1 dl) sugar
1 egg yolk
½ cup (1 dl) ground, blanched almonds
1½ cup (3½ dl) flour

Cream butter and sugar until light and fluffy. Add egg yolk, almonds and flour and mix thoroughly. Chill dough for 1 hour. Preheat oven to 325°. Use your thumbs to coat the inside of small fluted tins with dough. Put flour on your thumbs so the dough doesn't stick to them. Cook for 10 minutes or until light brown. Turn upside down on plain board. Bang tins lightly against board, to make sure that the tarts don't stick. Cool before removing tins. Serve plain or filled with jam and whipped cream.

Swedish specialities. The Norwegians have many more fish dishes on the Christmas menu than for example the Finns or the Danes. But in the whole of Scandinavia the food habits are changing. It's

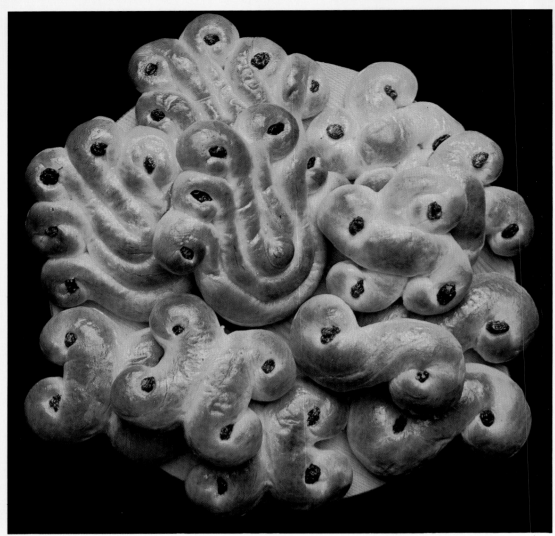

Lucia buns

no longer in line with today to have so many and
such rich dishes on the Christmas dinner-table
as before. It is not necessary either that all
the dishes are served at one and the same meal.

Lucia buns
20 buns

Lucia buns are made for the feast of St Lucie on December 13. St Lucie is a Catholic saint, a martyr from the 10th century who was blinded rather than betray her faith. How she came to be celebrated in Scandinavia no one knows for sure. Some say she was really a goblin queen worshipped long before the arrival of Christianity. Another story has it that the blinded maiden is a symbol of inner light, making her an appropriate saint to remember when the winter days are short.

At any rate, St Lucie celebrations are cherished all over Scandinavia. The feast of St Lucie is both solemn and commercial, funny and serious. The morning of the feast children get up very early and wake their parents with candles and buns. Young girls dressed in white walk in procession through homes, offices, hospitals and schools. They wear a wreath of fir or lingonberry twigs decorated with candles on their heads. Every town chooses one girl to represent St Lucie.

The deep yellow Lucia buns are appetizing to look at and good to eat. They contain saffron, an exotic spice. Their odd shape is an ancient one. Similarly shaped breads may have been used in sun or fertility rites in a pre-Christian era.

½ tsp saffron
1 package (20 g) of yeast
1 cup (2½ dl) milk
1 egg
1 stick (125 g) butter
⅔ cup (1½ dl) sugar
⅓ cup (1 dl) raisins
3¾—4 cups (9 dl—1 l) flour

Saffron gives off most of its flavor if it is ground. If you own a mortar, grind the fine threads together with 1 tbsp of sugar. You can also crush the saffron on a plate, using a table knife. Mix it with a little bit of sugar; the saffron threads are so fine that they'll stick to a knife or a plate, unless they are first mixed with some other ingredient.

Melt the butter over low heat. Pour the milk into the butter and heat the mixture to 85°. Crumble yeast in a large mixing bowl. Pour a little bit of the milk mixture over the yeast and stir until it is completely dissolved. Add the remaining milk. Now add saffron, sugar and raisins. Beat an egg lightly and mix it into the milk. Then gradually add flour. How to proceed from here, see basic recipe for yeast dough, page 93. When the dough has risen once and you've punched it down, shape Lucia buns (see picture) and let rise again. Brush with beaten egg and bake them for about 8 minutes in a hot oven, about 500°.

The shape of the Lucia buns dates back to fertility rites, performed by the Vikings. In December the days are short, and a sun-shaped bread may have been used in hopes of making the sun return.

Toffee
100 toffees

Home-made candy is part of a traditional Scandinavian Christmas. It can be made weeks in advance and kept—provided you have a good hiding place for it. The following recipes are easy to make, the candy is special and very good, and contrary to store bought varieties you know what ingredients went into it.

1 cup (2½ dl) sugar
1 cup (2½ dl) syrup
1 cup (2½ dl) whipping cream
3 tbsp butter
½ cup (1 dl) blanched, chopped almonds
approximately 100 tiny paper cups

Mix sugar, syrup, whipping cream and butter in a heavy pan. Simmer and stir for 35—45 minutes until a candy thermometer shows 240—250°. If you don't have a thermometer, test the mixture: drop a small amount of hot mixture into cold water. The mixture should form a semi-soft ball. Stir chopped almonds into the hot mixture and immediately pour about a teaspoon ful into each tiny paper cup.

Cream toffee
60—80 toffees

1¼ cup (3 dl) whipping cream
¾ cup (2 dl) table cream
1¼ cup (3 dl) sugar
¾ cup (2 dl) syrup
1 tsp vanilla

Mix all ingredients, except vanilla, in a heavy pan. Simmer and stir 35—45 minutes until a candy thermometer shows 240—250°. How to test the candy, see recipe beside. Stir in vanilla and pour mixture onto a cookie sheet or shallow baking pan, 8 × 12″ (20 × 30 cm). Let cool. Cut the candy into rectangular pieces, using a sharp oiled knife. Wrap pieces in foil or candy paper.

Scandinavians love traditions. At Christmas it seems as though they had not discarded a single ritual since the beginning of time. Under Scandinavian Christmas trees you are likely to find a

Chocolate balls
50 balls

4 oz (125 g) semi-sweet chocolate
2 tbsp water
3 egg yolks
4 oz (125 g) butter
⅓ cup (1 dl) confectioner's sugar
4 tbsp cocoa

Break chocolate into pieces and melt over low heat together with 2 tbsp of water. Remove from heat and add egg yolks, one at a time. Stir in butter and confectioner's sugar. Let cool. Form mixture into balls the size of a quarter and roll them in cocoa. Put balls into tiny paper cups and garnish with blanched almonds or nuts.

Glögg
10—12 servings

Glögg is the Swedish Christmas punch, hot, sweet, and sometimes very strong mulled wine. It's served throughout the month of December, and it's particularly popular for a Lucia party (see page 113). There are many variations of glögg, many different ways of spicing it. Sometimes it is made only of red wine, somewhat like a German Glühwein. You can add as much or as little aquavit (or vodka) as you like. Cardamon, cloves and cinnamon are standard ingredients, but you can add grated orange rind, lemon rind, nutmeg, chopped figs, or nuts.

2 bottles of burgundy or claret
1 small bottle (1 pint) of Swedish aquavit
  (or vodka, if you can't find aquavit)
½ lb (250 g) sugar
10 peeled cardamons
10 cloves
4 pieces of cinnamon
(2 tbsp of grated orange rind)

To serve with:
½ cup (1 dl) raisins
½ cup (1 dl) blanched almonds

Pour wine into kettle and add sugar and spices. Simmer slowly without boiling until sugar is completely dissolved. Add alcohol, heat, light with a match and let burn down. Serve in mugs or in cups with handles (it's very hot) together with almonds and raisins.

crib, the Christ child, Joseph and Mary, and the three wise men, all in good Christian order. But next to them there will be a goat made of straw. Perhaps the goat is a symbol of the devil; more

Gingerbread house

likely he is a left-over from pagan rites. Scandinavian Christmas tables and decorations are
full of "tomtenissar", goblins dressed in red
with beards and caps. They may have influenced

Gingerbread house

A gingerbread house is not as difficult to make as it may seem. You need a pattern cut out of cardboard (Scandinavians often keep the cardboard pattern from one Christmas to the next), some baking experience, and a good deal of patience and care.

1¼ cup (3 dl) brown sugar
¾ cup (2 dl) syrup
1 stick (125 g) butter
1 tbsp cinnamon
1 tbsp ground ginger
½ tbsp ground cloves
1¼ cup (3 dl) milk
1 tbsp baking soda
5—6 cups (1¼—1½ l) flour

Prepare dough one day in advance. Melt butter, syrup, sugar and spices over low heat in a large pan. Stir in milk and cool. Stir in baking soda. Reserve ½ cup (1 dl) flour. Add remaining flour to sugar mixture and blend into a soft dough. Sprinkle flour on top and chill till the next day.

Preheat oven to 345°. Knead dough on floured board. Divide into five even parts (you'll need one piece for the two sides, one for the front, one for the back, and two pieces for the roof). Sometimes it is recommended that you roll the dough directly on greased cookie sheets; try whichever method works best for you. Roll out dough ⅛" (3 mm) thick. It is essential to roll the dough evenly. It will rise once it's in the oven; any portion that's thicker than the rest will rise more, and you'll wind up with uneven pieces which won't fit together.

Now put the pattern pieces on top of the rolled out dough and cut around them with a sharp knife. You can either cut out windows and doors at this stage or draw them on the baked pieces with white icing later on. Cook for 10—15 minutes. As soon as you take the cookie sheets out of the oven check to make sure your pieces are even by putting the pattern on top of them again. As long as the pieces are hot you can still make corrections. Cut carefully around the edges with a sharp knife. Let cool.

the way we think of Santa Claus, but they belong to a pre-Christian era. In the countryside, a plate of rice porridge is still set out for the "tomtenissar" to enjoy on the Christmas Eve.

To decorate

Decorate pieces when they're completely cooled. Use store-bought white icing or make your own by mixing about 1¼ cup (3 dl) confectioner's sugar with 1 egg white. Add a drop or two of lemon juice if the icing isn't soft enough. Use a pastry bag with a small tip and decorate around doors and windows, or make a tiled roof, see picture. Let icing dry completely before putting the house together.

To put the house together

Use a cutting board, a tray or simply a piece of a wooden board covered with foil to build the house on. Melt 1 cup (2½ dl) sugar in a frying pan. Stir constantly over low heat until the sugar has dissolved completely. Keep it over very low heat. Now dip one side of the house in the hot sugar and press it together with the back of the house. Hold the pieces together at a right angle (draw a right angle on the base so that you know where to put the pieces) until the sugar has hardened and the pieces hold together. This takes a minute or two. Dip the other side into the sugar and press it firmly onto the back on your base. Then dip both sides of the front and put them on. If it is difficult to dip the piece on both sides, you can drop a little melted sugar along the sides of the house. Use a wooden spoon. Melted sugar is very hot and makes nasty burns. Drop sugar all around the upper edge of the house. Now dip the top edges of the two roof pieces into the melted sugar and press them together on the house. Hold firmly until the pieces stick.

Work fast and carefully. You'll succeed even if you've never done it before—but putting together a gingerbread house is *not* something children can help with. The sugar is hot and dangerous, the pieces quite brittle. If a piece breaks, it can be glued with melted sugar, or easier, taped together on the back. Scandinavians decorate their houses with twigs of fir, fir cones or lingonberry. You could also use holly, candles, tiny "tomtar" (Santas). Candy, however, is not part of a traditional gingerbread house.

For a real Scandinavian Christmas, light your house with candles and open some of the gifts after dinner on Christmas Eve. Traditionally, there should also be a poem on each package.

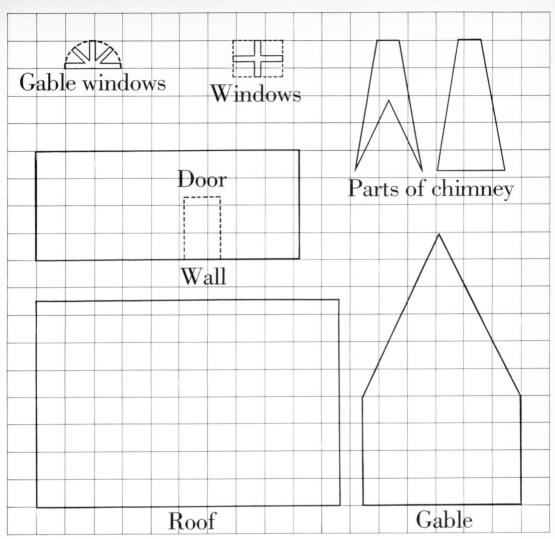

Gable windows

Windows

Door

Parts of chimney

Wall

Roof

Gable

Pattern for Gingerbread house
Cut out two pieces of all parts except for windows of which ten are needed

Conversion table

American and British weight measurements
1 ounze (oz) = 28 g
½ pound (lb) = 225 g
1 pound (lb) = 450 g
2 sticks butter = 225 g
1 package dry yeast = 1 cake compressed fresh yeast = ⅔ ounce = 20 g

American volume measurements
1 fluid ounce = 30 ml
1 cup = ½ pint = 8 fluid ounces = 2.4 dl
2 cups = 1 pint = 16 fluid ounces = 4.8 dl

British volume measurements
1 fluid ounce = 28 ml
1 cup = ½ pint = 10 fluid ounces = 2.8 dl
2 cups = 1 pint = 20 fluid ounces = 5.6 dl

Oven temperature	**F°**	**C°**
Very slow	250—275	125—135
Slow	300—325	150—175
Moderate	350—375	175—200
Hot	400—425	200—225
Very hot	450—475	225—250
Extremely hot	500—525	250—275

Index

89 Cardamon muffins
Kardemummamuffins (S)
Kardemomme-
muffins (N)
Kardemomme-
muffins (D)
Kardemumma-
muffinsit (F)

115 Chocolate balls
Chokladtryffel (S)
Sjokoladekuler (N)
Chokoladekugler (D)
Tryffelit (F)

107 Christmas dip
Dopp i grytan (S)
Mølje (N)
Dyp i gryten (D)
Kastinpata (F)

108 Christmas porridge
Risgrynsgröt (S)
Julegrøt (N)
Risengrød (D)
Riisipuuro (F)

103 Christmas sausage
Julkorv (S)
Julepølse (N)
Julepølse (D)
Joulumakkara (F)

107 Christmas spareribs
Ugnsstekta revbens-
spjäll (S)
Juleribbe (N)
Ribbensteg (D)
Paahtokylki (F)

110 Christmas stars
Julstjärnor (S)
Julestjerner (N)
Julestjerner (D)
Joulutähdet (F)

94 Cinnamon buns
Kanelsnurror (S)
Skillingsboller (N)
Hvedeboller med
kardemomme (D)
Kanelikiekot (F)

79 Cookies from Uppåkra
Uppåkrakakor (S)
Uppåkrakaker (N)
Uppåkrakager (D)
Uppåkran pikkuleivät (F)

70 Cranberry pears
Lingonpäron (S)
Pærer i tyttebærsaft (N)
Tyttebærpærer (D)
Puolukkapäärynät (F)

55 Crayfish
Kräftor (S)
Kreps (N)
Krebs (D)
Ravut (F)

114 Cream toffee
Gräddkarameller (S)
Fløtekarameller (N)
Flødekarameller (D)
Kermakaramellit (F)

15 Creamed kidney
Njursauté (S)
Nyrestuing (N)
Nyreragout (D)
Munuaishöystö (F)

49 Creamed perch
Stuvad abborre (S)
Stuet abbor (N)
Stuvet aborre (D)
Ahvenmuhennos (F)

36 Creamed potatoes
Stuvad potatis (S)
Potetstappe (N)
Stuvede kogte
kartofler (D)
Muhennetut keitetyt
perunat (F)

15 Creamed shrimp
Räkstuvning (S)
Rekestuing (N)
Rejestuvning (D)
Katkarapumuhennos (F)

66 Custard sauce
Vaniljsås (S)
Vaniljesaus (N)
Vanillesovs (D)
Vaniljakastike (F)

78 Danish almond cookies
Danska kransekager (S)
Kransekakestenger (N)
Kransekager (D)
Tanskalaiset
mantelileivät (F)

81 Danish apple cookies
Danska äppelbakelser (S)
Danske eplekaker (N)
Æblekager (D)
Tanskalaiset
omenaleivät (F)

26 Danish curried meatballs
Köttbullar i currysås (S)
Kjøttboller i karry-
saus (N)
Frikadeller i carry (D)
Lihapyörykät curry-
kastikkessa (F)

67 Danish fruit pudding
Rödgröd med flöde (S)
Rødgrøt med fløte (N)
Rødgrød med fløde (D)
Tanskalainen
hedelmäyanukas (F)

10 Danish herring salad
Dansk sillsallad (S)
Dansk sildesalat (N)
Dansk sildesalat (D)
Tanskalainen
sillisalaatti (F)

25 Danish meat patties
Danska frikadeller (S)
Danske frikadeller (N)
Frikadeller (D)
Tanskalaiset
lihapyörykät (F)

14 Danish omelet
Dansk äggkaka (S)
Dansk omelett (N)
Dansk æggekage (D)
Tanskalainen
munakas (F)

96 Danish pastry
Wienerbröd (S)
Wienerbrød (N)
Wienerbrød (D)
Wienerleivät (F)

38 Danish sauerkraut
Surkål (S)
Surkål på dansk (N)
Surkål (D)
Tanskalainen
hapankaali (F)

108 Danish spicy red cabbage
Dansk rödkål (S)
Dansk rødkål (N)
Rødkål (D)
Tanskalainen
punakaali (F)

13 Dilled herring
Sill i dill (S)
Sild i dill (N)
Sild i dild (D)
Tillisilli (F)

17 Dilled lamb or veal
Dillkött (S)
Kalve- eller lammekjøtt
i dillsaus (N)
Lamme- eller kalve-
frikassé (D)
Tilliliba (F)

57 Dumplings
Klimp (S)
Melboller (N)
Boller (D)
Kanssa (F)

98 Farm bread
Lantbröd (S)
Landbrød (N)
Landbrød (D)
Maalsaisileipä (F)

81 Farmer's cookies
Bondkakor (S)
Skiver (N)
Bondekager (D)
Talonpoikaiskakut (F)

27 Farmer's omelet
Bondomelett (S)
Bondeomelett (N)
Fransk bondeomelet (D)
Maalaismunakas (F)

79 Finnish cookies
Finska pinnar (S)
Finske brød (N)
Finske brød (D)
Murotangot (F)

63 Finnish cucumber soup
Finsk gurksoppa (S)
Finsk agurksuppe (N)
Finsk agurkesuppe (D)
Kurkkukeitto (F)

44 Fish au gratin
Fiskgratäng (S)
Gratinert fisk (N)
Fiskegratin (D)
Kuorrutettu kala (F)

50 Fish in aspic
Inkokt fisk (S)
Fiskekabaret (N)
Fisk i aspic (D)
Kala mausteliemessä (F)

51 Fish soufflée
Fisksufflé (S)
Fiskegrateng (N)
Fiskesoufflé (D)
Kalakohokas (F)

67 Fluffy berry pudding
Klappgröt (S)
Lett fruktgrøt (N)
Frugtbudding (D)
Vatkattu marjapuuro (F)

65 Fruit soup
Fruktsoppa (S)
Fruktsuppe (N)
Frugtsuppe (D)
Hedelmäkeitto (F)

111 Gingerbread cookies
Pepparkakor (S)
Pepperkaker (N)
Brune kager (D)
Piparkakut (F)

117 Gingerbread house
Pepparkakshus (S)
Pepperkakehus (N)
Brunekagehus (D)
Piparkakkutalo (F)

70 Ginger pears
Ingefärspäron (S)
Ingefærpærer (N)
Ingefærpærer (D)
Inkivääripäärvnät (F)

106 Glazed Christmas ham
Julskinka (S)
Glasert juleskinke (N)
Juleskinke (D)
Joulukinkku (F)

115 Glögg
Glögg (S)
Gløgg (N)
Gløgg (D)
Glögi (F)

80 Grandmother's hearts
Mormors hjärtan (S)
Mormors hjerter (N)
Mormors hjerter (D)
Isoäidin sydämet (F)

11 Grandmother's herring
Mormors sill (S)
Karrisild (N)
Bedstemors sild (D)
Isoäidin silli (F)

41 Grilled eel
Luad ål (S)
Grillet ål (N)
Grillstegt ål (D)
Ankerias skoone-
laisittain (F)

42 Grilled pike
Brasgädda (S)
Bakt fisk (N)
Grillstegt gedde (D)
Takkahauki (F)

102 Headcheese
Pressylta (S)
Sylte (N)
Flæskerullepølse (D)
Painesyltty (F)

47 Herring balls
Sillbullar (S)
Sildeboller (N)
Sildekarbonader (D)
Sillipyörykät (F)

104 Herring salad
Sillsallad (S)
Sildesalat (N)
Sildesalat (D)
Sillisalaatti (F)

11 Herring salad from Norway
Norsk sillsallad (S)
Norsk sildesalat (N)
Norsk sildesalat (D)
Norjalainen
sillisalaatti (F)

46 Herring with onion sauce
Stekt sill med löksås (S)
Stekt salt sild med
løksaus (N)
Stegt sild med
løgsovs (D)
Paistettu silli
sipulikastikkeessa (F)

50 Horse-radish cream
Pepparrotsgrädde (S)
Pepperrotssaus (N)
Peberrodsflødeskum (D)
Piparjuurikerma (F)

5 Jansson's temptation
Janssons frestelse (S)
Janssons fristelse (N)
Janssons fristelse (D)
Janssonin kiusaus (F)

87 Jelly roll
Rulltårta (S)
Rullekake (N)
Roulade (D)
Kääretorttu (F)

83 Jenny's favorites
Jennys favoritkakor (S)
Jennys favorittkaker (N)
Jennys kager (D)
Jennyn suosikkileivät (F)

59 Kale soup
Grönkålssoppa (S)
Grønnkålsuppe (N)
Grønkålsuppe (D)
Kaalikeitto (F)

21 Karelian steak
Karelsk stek (S)
Karelsk stek (N)
Karelsk ragout (D)
Karjalan paisti (F)

91 Kinuski torte
Kinuskitårta (S)
Kinuskiterte (N)
Kinuskitærte (D)
Kinuskikakku (F)

83 Lace cookies
Struvor (S)
Krabbelurer (N)
Kniplingekager (D)
Tippaleivät (F)

32 Lamb and cabbage stew
Får i kål (S)
Får i kål (N)
Får i kål (D)
Lammaskaali (F)

34 Lamb stew from Finland
Finsk lammstuvning (S)
Finsk lammestuing (N)
Finsk lammeragout (D)
Lammasmuhennos (F)

88 Layer cake from Finland
Potatistårta (S)
Finsk potetkake (N)
Finsk kartoffellag-
kage (D)
Perunakakku (F)

95 Lenten buns
Semlor (S)
Fastelavnsboller (N)
Simler (D)
Laskiaispullat (F)

27 Liver hash from Finland
Finsk leverlåda (S)
Finsk levergryte (N)
Finsk leverragout (D)
Maksalaatikko (F)

101 Liver paté
Leverpastej (S)
Leverpostei (N)
Leverpostej (D)
Maksapasteija (F)

113 Lucia buns
Lussekatter (S)
Lussekatter (N)
Lucia boller (D)
Joulupullat (F)

13 Marinated herring
Delikatessill (S)
Kryddersild (N)
Marinerede sild (D)
Marinoitu silli (F)

22 Marinated pot roast
Surstek (S)
Surstek (N)
Sursteg (D)
Hapanpaisti (F)

53 Marinated salmon
Gravad lax (S)
Gravet laks (N)
Gravad laks (D)
Tuoresuolainen lohi (F)

43 Marinated smelt
Ättikströmming (S)
Marinert stekt sild (N)
Stegte sild i marinade (D)
Etikkasilakat (F)

**37 Mashed potatoes-
rutabaga**
Rotmos (S)
Kålrabistappe (N)
Kålrabi- og kartoffel-
mos (D)
Juuressose (F)

6 Meatballs
Köttbullar (S)
Kjøttboller (N)
Kødboller (D)
Lihapyörykät (F)

26 Meat loaf
Färs i form (S)
Kjøttpudding (N)
Forloren hare (D)
Lihamureke (F)

77 Miss Pihlgren's pretzels
Madame Pihlgrens
kringlor (S)
Madame Pihlgrens
kringler (N)
Madame Pihlgrens
kringler (D)
Neiti Pihlgrenin
rinkilät (F)

**8 Mushroom-filled
tomatoes**
Champinjonfyllda
tomater (S)
Tomater fylt med
champignons (N)
Gratinerede tomater
med svampe (D)
Sienillä täytetyt
tomaatit (F)

58 Mushroom soup
Champinjonsoppa (S)
Champignongsuppe (N)
Champignonsuppe (D)
Herkkusienikeitto (F)

9 Mustard marinated smelt
Senapsgravad
strömming (S)
Sennepsgravet sild (N)
Gravad sild (D)
Sinappisuolattu
silakka (F)

125

62 Nettle soup
Nässelsoppa (S)
Neslesuppe (N)
Nældesuppe (D)
Nekkoskeitto (F)

82 Norwegian custard cakes
Norska linser (S)
Linser (N)
Norske linser (D)
Norjalaiset leivät (F)

52 Norwegian fish mousse
Fiskpudding (S)
Fiskepudding (N)
Norsk fiskebudding (D)
Kalavanukas (F)

77 Oatmeal cookies
Havreflarn (S)
Havremakroner (N)
Havrekager (D)
Kauralastut (F)

54 Old-fashioned dressing
Gammaldags salladssås (S)
Gammeldags salatdressing (N)
Gammeldags salatsovs (D)
Vanhanajan salaatinkastike (F)

7 Old man's delight
Gubbröra (S)
Ansjospytt (N)
Hakket æg og ansjos (D)
Anjoviskäriste (F)

82 Pancake cookies
Plättbakelser (S)
Pleskener (N)
Plättbakkelser (D)
Ohukaisleivokset (F)

75 Pancake torte
Pannkakstårta (S)
Pannekaketerte (N)
Pandekagetærte (D)
Kerrosräiskäleet (F)

74 Pancakes
Pannkakor (S)
Pannekaker (N)
Pandekager (D)
Räiskäleet ja
ohukaiset (F)

75 Pancakes from Finland
Finsk pannkaka (S)
Finsk pannekake (N)
Finske pandekager (D)
Soumalainen
pannukakku (F)

33 Pancakes with bacon
Fläskpannkaka (S)
Fleskepannekake (N)
Pandekager med
flæsketerninger (D)
Silavapannukakut (F)

38 Pickled cucumber
Pressgurka (S)
Sursyltede slange-
agurker (N)
Agurkeskiver i
eddikelage (D)
Mausterkurkut (F)

104 Pickled herring
Glasmästarsill (S)
Glassmestersild (N)
Glarmestersild (D)
Laisimestarin silli (F)

10 Pickled smelt
Falska sardiner (S)
Falske sardiner (N)
Falske sardiner (D)
Tomaattisilakat (F)

49 Pike with horse-radish
Pepparrotsgädda (S)
Pepperrotsgjedde (N)
Gedde med peberrod (D)
Piparjuurihauki (F)

30 Piroskhi
Pirog (S)
Pirog (N)
Pirog (D)
Piirakat (F)

**34 Potatoes à la Hassel-
backen**
Hasselbackspotatis (S)
Hasselbackpoteter (N)
Kartofler à la
Hasselback (D)
Hasselbackin
perunat (F)

35 Potato dumplings
Kroppkakor (S)
Potetkroketter (N)
Svenske kartoffel-
kager (D)
Perunakakut (F)

67 Prune soufflée
Katrinplommon-
sufflé (S)
Sviskesufflé (N)
Svedskesoufflé (D)
Luumukohokas (F)

90 Puff pastry torte
Tusenbladstårta (S)
Tusenbladsterte (N)
Tusindbladstærte (D)
Tuhatlehtikakku (F)